Shades of Belonging

Shades of Belonging

Conversations with Australian Jews

NEER KORN

HarperCollins*Publishers*

HarperCollins*Publishers*

Published by HarperCollins*Religious*
A member of HarperCollins*Publishers* (Australia) Pty Limited Group
Level 3/150 Jolimont Rd.
East Melbourne, Victoria 3002
http://www.harpercollins.com.au

HarperCollins*Publishers*
25 Ryde Road, Pymble, Sydney NSW 2073, Australia
31 View Road, Glenfield, Auckland 10, New Zealand
77–85 Fulham Palace Road, London W6 8JB, United Kingdom
Hazelton Lanes, 55 Avenue Road, Suite 2900, Toronto, Ontario M5R 3L2
and 1995 Markham Road, Scarborough, Ontario M1B 5M8, Canada
10 East 53rd Street, New York NY 10032, USA

National Library of Australia Cataloguing-in-Publication data:

Korn, Neer.
    The Australian Jew.
    ISBN 1 86371 731 5.
    1. Jews - Australia - Interviews. 2. Jews - Australia -
    History. 3. Immigrants - Australia - Interviews. I. Title.
994.004924

Cover photographs: The Photo Library/Ken Fisher
Printed in Australia by Griffin Press Pty Ltd, Adelaide on 79gsm Bulky Paperback.

5 4 3 2 1
97 98 99 00 01

To my grandparents
Leo & Rina
Pinchas & Miriam (deceased)

Contents

Preface

Many books have been written about Australian Jewish history; mostly factual accounts of the Jewish community, its issues, personalities and impacting events. This book does not aim to offer a comprehensive understanding of history. Rather, it is the story of the community seen through the eyes of its members and told in their words. It is a snapshot of a community, capturing a moment in time.

Each of the people in this book has a different story to tell. As a group, they were selected to reflect the diversity of the community; the many individual experiences and expressions which collectively provide some understanding of it. The interviews are divided into three sections: those born before or during the Second World War, the post-1945 generation, and those born since the social revolutions of the 1960s. They show the contrasts and continuities of Jewish life throughout the world in the twentieth century, with a strongly Australian inflection.

I am grateful to the people who agreed to be interviewed for this book, inviting me into their homes and offices with tape recorder in hand. Following an interview I would often feel a deep sense of humility, having been permitted to enter the interviewee's life, for a short while. I have intentionally left the interviews raw, with only minimal editing, so that to read them is to listen to a story being told as if the readers themselves were in the same room as the interviewees. Many of the interviewees use Yiddish and Hebrew words which have not been directly translated within their stories. However, readers will find all foreign words, together with many other names of people and places, defined, in the extensive glossary at the back of the book.

To represent the Jewish community in its fullness would require a book of thousands of interviews, for every story is unique in its own right. The challenge of selecting 28 as representatives of the Australian Jewish experience has been a difficult one, relying on the advice and suggestions of many people. Ultimately, some readers may notice omissions or under-representation of certain experiences and backgrounds, many due to circumstance.

My interest in the Australian Jewish community is long-standing and somewhat ingrained. I am fascinated by the survival of Jewish identity despite the many attempts at its obliteration. I am deeply affected by the dedication demonstrated by the forebears of Jews alive today to maintain the values, customs, traditions and beliefs of Judaism.

I would like to thank Vic Alhadeff , Rabbi Raymond Apple, Alexis Goodstone, Anthea Kessel, Robert Marjenberg, Myer Samra and Shira Sebban for their much appreciated advice. Also thanks to Cathy Jenkins and Susannah Burgess, respectively publisher and editor at HarperCollins*Religious*, for their support and encouragement. And finally, thanks also to all those around me who patiently listened to endless stories during the writing of this book.

Not all those who wander are lost
— JRR Tolkien

Introduction

Origins

Sarolta Budai was not enthusiastic about relaying her story for this book. She did not regard it as remarkable, explaining that 'there are many more like it, many people with similar experiences'. Here was a woman who had spent several years devoured by the Holocaust, at one stage wiping blood and body parts from ambulances for Dr Mengele in Auschwitz. She had witnessed her mother being selected to die in the gas chambers and had survived only to experience life under communism, which saw her husband jailed for eighteen months. Not remarkable, indeed!

And yet, there are many more stories like Sarolta's in Sydney's Jewish community, Australia being home to, proportionally, the largest number of Holocaust survivors outside Israel. It is a community of refugees, many from Hungary, who had escaped the looming dangers of World War II in Europe, and of communism following the war. It is also a community of these people's children, whose experiences were passed on from parent to child, like a genetic code, with its history of suffering, loss and survival remain embedded in the psyche.

The Jewish community here is also as old as white settlement in Australia, with Esther Abrahams and at least 15 other Jews transported on the First Fleet in 1788. It is a community whose members went wherever work was available, becoming lawyers and merchants, but also farmers and country store keepers, as attested by the many Jewish gravestones and synagogue remnants in country towns.

Today, the Jewish community is largely wealthy and successful but also has its share of poverty and social problems. 'I had only recently realised that we have a lot of local needs as well,' Eva, who is President of Jewish Community Services, explains. 'The perception of the Jews is obviously of success and privilege, and that exists. Only we're not immune, be it from domestic violence, drug abuse, alcoholism, poverty, disability, mental and physical ailments.'

More recently, Australia has become home to a large South African Jewish population, which has soared in the last two decades to account for 10 per cent of the community. Extremely resourceful, South African Jews have succeeded in recreating their closely-knit community life, almost transplanting it from Johannesburg and Cape Town to Sydney's North Shore. 'When we arrived you couldn't buy a *Rosh Hashana* card in St Ives,' says Vic Alhadeff, Editor of the *Australian Jewish News*, 'But today there is a whole section in the Shopping Village saying "Jewish cards", and that is obviously a function of the South African immigration of the last decade.'

As they settle into Australian life and reap the financial rewards offered by Australia's culture of opportunity, some of the South African Jews are gradually joining the rest of the community and moving towards the more expensive real estate of Sydney's Eastern Suburbs, where Bellevue Hill, Vaucluse, Rose Bay, Bondi and Dover Heights are home to much of the Jewish population.

Like any newly arrived immigrant group, the Jews headed to where others of the same origins resided. The ensuing creation of a complex communal infrastructure consisting of synagogues and temples, schools, organisations, services and social clubs, has ensured that the population remains centred on these suburbs. And likewise, these have developed, albeit to a lesser degree, on the Upper North Shore, in particular St Ives, where the Kehilat Mesada Synagogue, which has grown from 100 to 500 families in one decade, is 90 per cent South African.

The most recent substantial addition to the community's multicultural composition are the immigrants from the former Soviet Union, trickling here when immigration from the Soviet Union was sporadic and soaring when the floodgates opened following Gorbachev's glasnost. Permission to enter Australia is more difficult now with stricter immigration guidelines, but thanks to the tireless efforts of Jewish Community Services, many of those with families living in Australia are able to be reunited with them. For Ukraininan Zina Satanovskaia, reuniting with her sister in Australia also provided a better environment for her severely intellectually disabled son.

As a group, the Russians are mostly poor, their previously highly regarded skills not accredited in Australia and their monetary assets few. Hence, home for many has become the housing commission apartments of Redfern and Newtown, where they represent a visible enclave of their own. 'But we are not poor, we can have everything necessary for our lives,' is Zina's optimistic outlook.

The majority of the Russian Jews do not identify with Judaism in a strong sense, having been unsure of their Jewish identity in a country where living fully as a Jew was not possible under communism.

Efforts to integrate the Russians into the Jewish community have been in operation for some years and, as they settle into the work force and are able to afford apartments, they have moved to the Bondi area, integrating with increasing success. There are social functions, synagogue services, English classes and, from time to time, Russian-language publications which cater for them. The Bondi area also boasts Russian video rental shops, restaurants and halls for their frequent celebrations. In addition, many of their children attend the private Jewish day schools, often at reduced fees. The motive for many in sending their children to Jewish schools may be the opportunity to offer them the quality of a private education, being largely suspicious of government-run systems. The result, however, is children who are introducing Jewish traditions and teaching to homes which have been largely devoid of them.

The successful integration of Russian Jews into Jewish communal life in Sydney would seal the efforts of the campaign for their freedom in the 70s and 80s. The fate of Russian Jews inspired massive rallies and unprecedented communal mobilisation, with the call to the Russian authorities to 'Let my people go'. Diane Shteinman was a leading activist in the Soviet Jewry campaign. She tells her story here.

There are also the Sephardim, Jews from communities across Asia and around the Mediterranean basin. Their customs, practices, prayers and tunes differ from those of Ashkenazi Jewry (of Northern European background). Some of the communities which identify as Sephardim have histories that reach back to biblical times.

Like its Ashkenazi counterpart, Sephardi Jewry has undergone enormous upheaval in the 20th century. The Ladino culture, which flourished in the Balkans for nearly 500 years following the expulsion of Jews from Spain in 1492, was all but annihilated during the Holocaust when Southern Europe was conquered by the Nazis and their allies. Meanwhile, those communities which were long established in Arab countries faced uncertainty and deportation in the years following the founding of the State of Israel in 1948.

Myer Samra, a lawyer and anthropologist, who is originally from Iraq, describes in his interview a Jewish community once integral to Iraqi society. 'At the beginning of the century, Jews began moving out of their quarter, into the Christian Quarter of Baghdad, building finer, bigger houses, and moving into the suburbs.' They left, however, in a very short space of time, and en masse, in 1950 and 1951. Israel took in about 120,000 people from Iraq in that one year. Myer says 'It would have been like the entire Jewish community in Australia packing up and saying goodbye.'

When Sephardi Jews from Egypt, Asia and the Middle East sought to settle in Australia after the Second World War, they were confronted by the White Australia Policy which intended to restrict the entry of non-whites into the country, and also by local Jews of largely Ashkenazi background, some of whom found it difficult to accept that these people, often of a more swarthy complexion, who had not the slightest understanding of the Yiddish language and many of whom came from countries outside Europe, could in fact be Jews.

Today, however, there are no less than five Sephardi congregations operating in Sydney, several of them supported by the steady stream of young Israeli travellers visiting Australia. While seeking to maintain their own tradition and identity, the Sephardi Jews have also successfully integrated into the broader Sydney Jewish community.

The community is also home to several B'nai Menashe, members of a group from the states of Manipur and Mizoram in India — who consider themselves descendants of the biblical tribe of Manasseh —

and to several members of Beta Israel — the Jews of Ethiopia (believed by some to be remnants of the Tribe of Dan) who had long been separated from other Jews and had developed their own unique traditions. Miriam Frommer, a B'nai Menashe who came to Sydney following her marriage to Myer, grew up surrounded by Jewish ritual. 'When I was born, my dad already observed *Shabbat*, so I've been brought up as a *Shabbat* keeper.'

And, of course, there are the Israelis living in Sydney, of whom I am one. Although the thinking has now changed, their arrival on our shores, until recently, was met with mixed emotion. Certainly, they are Jews, it was reasoned, but they left the State of Israel, an act labelled *Yerida* — literally, 'to descend'. There was even a time when Israel's diplomatic representatives would refuse to embrace them, attend their celebrations or address their Hebrew radio programs. Much has eased and over the years they have developed their own associations, celebrations and religious services. There was even, for a brief period, a Hebrew language supplement to the weekly *Australian Jewish News*. Many Israelis identify with Israeli culture only, with no involvement in the religious or charitable institutions of the Jewish community. But here too, where their children attend Jewish day schools, the parents are encouraged to embrace communal life.

If Australia is regarded as a multicultural society then its Jewish community is a microcosm of ethnic origins.

Reform and Orthodox — under one roof

Other than region of origin, the clearest division in Judaism today is between Reform and Orthodox. There is a joke sporadically heard in the Jewish community that a Jew who finds himself cast away on an island would build an Orthodox synagogue and a Reform temple, so that one can be the place he does not go. For most Sydney Jews, their identification with Reform or Orthodox seldom extends beyond the bounds of their temple or synagogue, although divisive issues do arise occasionally.

These two streams of Judaism differ in their belief about the authenticity of the Written Law, the Five Books of Moses, and the Oral Law, the body of interpretation and application of these laws. Central to Orthodoxy is the divine source of these laws: From this comes the lifestyle and dietary regulations, to which they adhere.

Reform Judaism, on the other hand, believes that humans wrote the Torah, albeit inspired by God. The laws for them are a guideline to living, requiring adjustment to be relevant to modern times.

Major-General Paul Cullen, whose father and grandfather were presidents of the Great Synagogue in Sydney, maintains that it was he who first introduced Reform Judaism to Sydney, in 1937. 'What I liked about the idea of liberal Judaism is that I don't speak Hebrew, I know some songs and hymns, but they didn't mean much to me and they were an impediment to my Jewish faith. Within a year we built a temple and we raised a lot of money for it, and we never had any trouble getting people. In fact we were surprised how many people wanted to join us.'

Ideologically, the two theological beliefs are at loggerheads. In reality, however, they coexist mostly amicably in Australia, where moderate leaders have ensured that differences pale in relation to the commonalities between all Jews. It may also be due to the unique membership ratio of synagogues and temples in Australia. Whereas most American Jews identify with the Reform or Conservative movements, in Australia it is Orthodoxy which dominates, with far greater numbers of synagogues and memberships. Although only an estimated 10 per cent of Jews would regard themselves as observant or Orthodox Jews, there are over 30 orthodox congregations in Sydney, each playing host to a cast of regular worshippers on Friday nights, *Shabbat* mornings and festivals, and to much greater numbers during life-cycle events such as weddings, bar mitzvahs and deaths. In comparison, there are only two Reform temples. It is the Orthodox Judaism, therefore, with which Australian Jews have historically identified, and still do.

And yet, Australian Jews are largely non-Orthodox in practice, not adhering fully to the strict laws such as those prohibiting driving on the Sabbath and festivals and the dietary laws. By American definition they would be Conservative Jews, whose position on observance of practices is somewhere between Reform and Orthodox. Sydney is home to a single Conservative style congregation; a part of the Reform temple, it is among the fastest growing congregations in Sydney.

'Traditional' is perhaps the most apt word to describe Sydney's Jews. They regard Judaism from a cultural rather than theological perspective, embracing a sense of community most of all. Yet twice a year, on *Rosh Hashana* and *Yom Kippur*, they attend synagogues and temples in such high numbers that these are filled to capacity and employ overflow services to accommodate the numbers.

The other ritual that is overwhelmingly observed is *Pesach*, or Passover, with its *seder* or feast celebrating the liberation of the Israelites from slavery in Egypt, taking place in most Jewish homes. Ninety-eight year-old Melita Stillchweig recalls preparations for the festival as a child in Germany. 'You can't imagine how much cleaning went on before *Pesach*. Every dish and saucepan was scraped and cleaned before putting away. Silver was boiled, glass stood for three days in water. We didn't feel it as restriction or an unpleasant duty — it was all a matter of course.'

The festival of *Channukah*, marking the Maccabees' overthrow of their Greek rulers, is celebrated with public menora-lighting ceremonies. Giant candelabras are erected in central locations and lit usually by public figures. This is often the work of the Lubavitch community, a mere 400 families in Sydney whose influence and impact on the community far exceeds their numbers.

The Lubavitch Orthodox follow the teachings of their spiritual leader or Rebbe, the last of whom died in 1994 at the age of 92. Their name reflects the Ukrainian village in which the movement began in the 18th century. The reverence in which he was, and still is, held, is prominently and outwardly displayed by the movement's adherents. For example, his photograph may be found hanging on the walls of Lubavitch homes and offices.

The Lubavitch do not differ from other Orthodox Jews in their belief in the fundamental tenets of Judaism, although they would regard other Orthodox Jews as being lax in many areas. Sydney was even serviced for a long time by two *kashrut* authorities (the religious bodies responsible for deeming food products, meat and restaurant kitchens to be prepared or operating under kosher guidelines). These have since been amalgamated, typifying the community's overall success in retaining unity when differences arise.

The Lubavitch have built a collection of Jewish institutions, including the Yeshiva learning centre, primary and high schools and rabbinical college. They are loud and proud, bringing Judaism to the people through public events, lectures and celebrations. They express their pride in Judaism in a manner so public that it seemed uncomfortable, perhaps even intimidating, to the largely European congregations accustomed to a quieter expression of identification. 'I'm not in favour' says Kitty Finger, a traditional Jew with a keen interest in alternative beliefs, 'of members from the Orthodox community going on the street wearing *talitim* (prayer shawls) or *shtreimels* (round fur hats) ... I feel as a people we already have enough problems without attracting more attention and demonstrating our cultural differences in a country where we are in the minority and which is for many of us an adoptive country.'

While endorsement of their public talks, concerts, dinners and religious carnivals has been widespread, the line was crossed several years ago with the death of the Lubavitch Rebbe and claims by some of his followers that he was the Messiah. The common view among Lubavitch adherents is that he had the qualities necessary to be a Messiah, but he could only be the Messiah if everyone accepted that he was. The messianic notion is a central tenet of Orthodox Judaism; prayers are said daily to expedite the Messiah's arrival. A billboard and bus advertising campaign was developed several years ago urging Jews to hasten the arrival of the Messiah through good deeds, or *mitzvot*.

The acceptance of the Lubavitch may also be due, among other things, to the numerous synagogues employing Lubavitch rabbis. With a large number of children, most of whom are encouraged to become rabbis, the Lubavitch provide, more or less, the only local rabbinical replenishment, because the pulpit is not the career of choice for the modern Orthodox. Most of Sydney's Orthodox synagogues employ home-grown rabbis of the Lubavitch community.

Interestingly, financial support for the Lubavitch movement comes largely from wealthy secular Jews — partly as a religious insurance policy. The continuity of Judaism and the curtailing of assimilation are the Jewish community's greatest challenge, and the Orthodox are seen by many as the vanguards of Jewish practice. 'To me there is great value in Orthodoxy,' explains Professor Ron Penny, an identifying Jew and proclaimed atheist. 'They are the curators of the Jewish faith and the Jewish traditions.'

For most Australian Jews, their strong sense of identification is based more on community and a shared heritage than on the laws of Judaism.

To Australian Jews, the Holocaust, along with the birth of the State of Israel, were formative events in defining their Jewish identity. These two diametrically opposed events, the obliteration of European Jewry, who had nowhere to go, and the creation of a permanent home for the Jewish people, mark this community. 'I think about what they went through a lot,' explains Jackie Reed, a 30-year-old whose parents were Hungarian refugees. 'I'm always thinking I have such a good life, such a lucky life, and you feel a certain amount of guilt that your parents didn't have that and now if you have problems of any sort, they're a bit diminished by the problems they had at your age and that's something I've had to get over, that feeling of guilt and not having suffered as they have, so if I'm feeling depressed, what am I feeling depressed about, not having to worry about survival?'

Many Jews express their identity through participation in the community's numerous organisations, which play host to thousands of volunteers and committee members. Such high participation rates and constant generous responses to appeals have allowed the community to build large, sophisticated and efficient organisations.

There are also many people whose Judaism is felt through a Jewish circle of friends, or participation in traditional Friday night dinners. Juanita Stein expands on her sense of identity, 'I feel most Jewish around the family — occasionally we have Friday night dinner. I'm not very Zionistic, not very religious, not very anything. But I'll turn on the news and see five kids killed, my age, in Israel, and I'd feel extremely Jewish all of a sudden.'

And there are the many who have abandoned Judaism for its lack of relevance to their lives, feeling no need to express their Jewishness. As Tom Reed, a 31-year-old puts it, 'I'm hoping that peace in the world comes when everyone marries everyone, there is no "this is a Catholic or a Jew", they're just people.'

There are those who have converted to Judaism. Each has individual reasons for making such a decision. Judaism is not a proselytising religion. Indeed, those wishing to convert are officially dissuaded several times from doing so before being accepted. Vaughan Cobbin changed his name to Gamliel following conversion from Christianity several years ago. He was originally drawn to the sense of strong values which he observed in Jewish families. 'At that time, I was also noticing the things that were missing from my family environment — that there's got to be something about the way these people live, there was a big family connection in their lives ... How we behave towards our fellow human beings is incredibly important, how we behave in the world, how we behave as Jews. Being Jewish is being alive.'

The differing nature of approaches to Jewish laws makes the conversion process the most dividing issue between Orthodox and Reform. At the heart of the matter is the destiny of the children of Reform converts, who may not have undergone conversion in accordance with *Halachah*, or Jewish law. From an Orthodox perspective, their children's Judaism is therefore questionable. Paul Benjamin, for example, is a Jewish studies teacher whose mother converted through Reform Judaism when she married his father. He shares his thoughts on his Judaism and the possible implications of his mother's conversion in his interview.

The Orthodox are therefore seeking a uniform standard for conversions which does not deviate from Jewish law. By definition, the Orthodox cannot actually change Jewish laws which are prescribed by God, and they fear that changes adopted in Reform Jewish practice are detrimental to Jewish continuity. 'The more you water down your *Yiddishkeit* the less chance you have of having a Jewish great-grandchild,' says Henry Kinstlinger. 'You look at Reform. How many Reform great-great-grandparents are there?'

The Reform, however, see themselves as offering a connection to Judaism for those Jews who would otherwise not affiliate with Orthodoxy. 'I think there are a lot of people who identify as Orthodox Jews but who don't meet the standards of Orthodox Judaism,' says Paul Benjamin. 'It's not necessarily a criticism ... but I don't think the modern Orthodox Jewry today, where people identify with the movement but fail to live up to the basic ideals of it, I don't think that's a sustainable situation.'

Finally, there are also the Jews who have converted to other religions. Interestingly, Jews may be found in large proportions among many religious groups and sects throughout Australia. Ella Dreyfus explains their motivation, 'There were years ... when I went searching. I went to Indian gurus, I went to Japan, to monasteries, did that classic search that ex-Catholics and Jews do.'

A well-oiled machine

Each year, the community's roof body, the NSW Jewish Board of Deputies, the voice of a conglomeration of 65 organisations, synagogues and schools, publishes a community diary, or Yellow Pages. Leafing through this booklet, one is struck by the sheer number and scope of organisations servicing a mere 40,000 people.

There are organisations to cater for every need of the community, including religious groups and authorities, schools, educational facilities, aged care and health services, welfare services, social groups, sports clubs, kosher facilities, Zionist organisations and fundraising bodies. Among them are specialised services such as one catering for single people who enjoy the outdoors, the weekly readings of the *Australian Jewish News* on radio for blind people, those dedicated to exploring the Jewish history of Australia, and the Jewish secular humanists.

Two of the largest organisations are the Board of Deputies, the parliament and public face of the community, and the State Zionist Council, the organisation linking Australian Jews to Israel. The passion which Australian Jews feel towards Israel is both a result of the Holocaust, when Jews had nowhere to turn, and the birth of the Jewish state. So powerful is this connection that, during the 1967 Six Day War, many young Australian Jews flew to Israel as volunteers, to provide necessary agricultural labour, while the Israelis were on active duty. They responded to a crisis which they, and many Jews around the world, saw as a danger to the very existence of the State of Israel.

Generations of young people have grown up in Zionist youth movements, which have produced the highest rate (per capita) of *aliyah*, or emigration to Israel, in the free world. Most Australian Jews have visited Israel at least once, with many people going on educational tours. The provision of an 'Israel experience', particularly for young Jews of school age, is high on the community's agenda.

The organised raising and distribution of funds is an area in which the community has excelled. Alongside the Board of Deputies and State Zionist Council are the fundraising bodies, the Jewish Communal Appeal and the United Israel Appeal. The former collects funds for local Jewish needs, raising and distributing funds on behalf of many of the community's organisations, who would otherwise do so individually and less effectively. The latter raises money for projects in Israel and the rescue of Jewish refugees. There is also the smaller Jewish National Fund, raising money for environmental projects in Israel. These two large organisations have set calendar periods for their respective campaigns, marked by large fundraising functions popularly supported by the community. The annual published list of donors numbers in the thousands.

In recent years, debate has arisen as to where the greater need lies and whether more funds should be retained in Australia rather than channelled to Israel. High rates of assimilation and intermarriage in America (around 50 to 60 per cent) alarm Australian Jews who fear such figures here. Australian Jews feel safer, however, due to the Jewish day school system which is estimated to provide a Jewish education to some 60 per cent of the community's children. This is in addition to various extra curricular classes available to those in state and non-Jewish schools through the NSW Board of Jewish Education.

But the running of schools is expensive, and many Jewish parents cannot afford the high fees. So for the schools to fulfil the community's pledge that no Jewish child should be denied a Jewish education, many believe the funds sent to Israel should remain in Australia and be put into subsidising Jewish education.

The community is serviced by a single newspaper, the *Australian Jewish News*, now owned by a family which is one of a handful of the community's major benefactors. These wealthy people, whose names may be found among the columns of *Business Review Weekly*'s annual list of Australia's richest 200, built their fortunes in many cases from the ashes of Holocaust, having arrived in Australia as penniless refugees. Their donations of large sums to a wide-ranging gamut of Jewish and other charities are responsible for the community's infrastructure, as attested by plaques of recognition on the walls of many institutions. In their absence, the community would be stripped to a minimum.

Too comfortable?

As a period in Jewish history, the story of the Australian Jews is one of unusual freedom. They have been welcomed into all levels of Australian life, from its boardrooms to the courts, the army, parliament and, twice, to the highest office of Governor-General. Among the Australian people, the Jews have been able to enjoy both commercial and professional opportunities and the freedom to express their identity.

Australia is not, however, completely devoid of anti-Semitism, and this is something of which the Jewish community remains wary. The perpetrators of a spate of arson attacks on synagogues in recent years — particularly during the Gulf War — have yet to be found. Broken windows and daubings on Jewish institutions and shopfronts are a common occurrence, and many conspicuously dressed religious Jews will speak of frequent verbal assaults. The Jewish community, alone among Australia's religions and belief systems, requires armed security guards to protect congregations while members worship inside. On a day-to-day level, however, Australian Jews are largely unaffected by anti-Semitism, and violent personal attacks are virtually unheard of.

Paradoxically, the great freedoms offered by Australian life also include the invitation to assimilate, to blend into Australian culture and abandon Jewish practices in the process. To resist this is one of the primary concerns of the Jewish community. Most Jews regard as central their role of ensuring the continuity of the Jewish people. Ron Penny describes this drive, 'If you ask me what the motivation for my Jewish identity is, part of it is respect for my forefathers and foremothers, because they died for their Jewish identity. So it's hard for me to reject it. I fear subsequent generations will feel differently.'

Indeed, for many young people, that connection and sense of identification has loosened. As is true of other Western countries, young people have mostly relegated major religions to the past, as antiquated belief systems which are out of touch with modernity. A lifestyle which dictates what foods may be eaten and the requirement to pray three times per day is not seen as compelling next to television, parties, music, movies, careers, relationships and so on. For some young people, New Age philosophies satisfy a spiritual thirst, but for most, spiritual apathy fills the gap. Judaism does not have a central role in their lives, particularly those who did not experience much of it at home. 'If you said to me "what is Judaism?" that would be too difficult to answer. It's very undefinable,' is how Juanita Stein puts it. 'I just believe in so many different things. It's such a cliched answer and you've probably heard it a million times before from peers, but I'm extremely spiritual much more than I am religious ... Judaism can't be the whole truth because it doesn't free people ... No religion frees people. If all you're working for is the next life you miss out on this one.' Children who grew up in homes largely void of any Jewish traditions claim hypocrisy, for example, when their parents disapprove of their relationship with a non-Jewish partner.

Many young Jews would nevertheless still prefer to marry someone Jewish, some for reasons of convenience 'because there's a lot they would understand that somebody who wasn't wouldn't. There's just something undefinable,' says Juanita.

Young women, particularly, pose a challenge for the Jewish community to sustain their interest and involvement. For many, the laws of Orthodoxy are deemed sexist, interpreted at a time when women had no rights. Peta Jones Pellach, a Jewish educator, for example, is one of a growing number of women seeking equality within the bounds of *Halachah*, or Jewish law, without compromising it.

But for a growing number of women, Orthodoxy does not effectively answer their call, and many are turning to the Reform temples where they are offered outward expressions of equality.

Last word

When word broke of the assassination of Israeli Prime Minister Yitzhak Rabin, on November 4, 1995, the news spread in the community faster then the media could relay the message. That evening, the community gathered in a packed Great Synagogue to experience the tragedy together. And when the bridge collapsed at the Macabiah games, on July 14, 1997, killing two Australian Jews and injuring 70, everyone seemed to know someone involved.

It has been suggested that every human being on the planet is related to every other human being by six degrees of separation at most. Part of the Jewish experience, for those who identify with the community, is a far smaller degree of separation. Regardless of their background, religious affiliation, age and profession, there seems to be an inherent connection between Jews, which is not always easy to articulate. Yet it is this connection, in fact, beyond all the categories of religion and country of origin, which defines the Jewish community.

IN THE SHADOW
OF DESTRUCTION:
VOICES IN THE
AFTERMATH OF WAR

A Survivor's Tale

Sabina Van Der Linden

Having survived the war on her wits, in later years, Sabina began speaking of her experiences in order to educate the young. I meet Sabina in her stylish home, with carefully selected artworks decorating the walls. Surrounded by her three cats, we sit at the dining table.

I am a child of the Holocaust. I survived in Poland and am the only survivor from my entire family.

My parents had a wholesale business and my father was also the managing director of a commercial bank. We were fairly comfortable and fairly assimilated. I was aware that we were Jewish because we celebrated Jewish holidays but I don't know whether we had a kosher home. I did eat ham, for instance, and had school on Saturday and we spoke Polish at home.

Life was very comfortable until 1939 when the war started. We were occupied by the Russians and our home was nationalised; we were declared enemies of the state. My father was arrested and imprisoned but he was released after a while. In the first few months, there were many adjustments which had to be made. I lived before in a very nice home, I had a governess, and all that had to go. We feared being sent to Siberia, so we used to hide and sleep in different homes until it all settled down. In a certain way, we were happy because my mother worked full-time before and we were brought up by the governess and suddenly my mother was at home. It's amazing how you adapt to circumstances, if they are fairly reasonable, of course.

The war between Germany and Russia broke out in 1941, and within three days of the Nazis occupying the town, the first pogrom took place. The change was just incredible, there was nothing to compare it to. I was eleven years old. It was the most horrific, terrifying experience. Murder, killing, maiming, raping. That was the first taste of what was in store for us. Afterwards, there were many very well-organised deportations. One was never safe in such a climate of fear. Then came the order to wear a yellow star. The killings continued, catching people in the street, people disappearing, taken to the forest and killed there. People were not fully aware as yet of what would become of the Jewish population. And despite everything that was happening, somehow people still held on to a sense of hope, that things would stabilise.

But things did not settle, of course. After the Wannsee conference of 1942, in which the Nazis formulated the final solution to European Jewry, it became clear to us that very little hope remained for the future of the Jews. On the 6th, 7th and 8th of August of that year, approximately 8,000 Jews from our city were rounded up and deported. At that time, my family was in hiding and were discovered. My father and brother were rounded up and taken away and I was taken away with my mother along with many others to a local cinema, used as a holding centre by the Nazis. I was desperately holding onto her hand but along with several other girls was taken away to another place and was put to work sorting through the belongings of deported Jews. I was never to see my mother again, they were all transported elsewhere. It was only some weeks later that we learnt they were sent to Belzec, an extermination camp. Several days later, I was allowed to return to our house and was incredibly happy to find that my father and brother were already there.

Two months later, the Nazis created a ghetto, forcing the remaining Jewish population to move into it. Concentrating the Jews in such a small area provided the Nazis with efficient means of controlling the Jewish population of Boryslaw. Within ten days, a labour camp was established in our city and all those able to work were taken there, with only the elderly, sick and the very young remaining in the ghetto. The ghetto was later liquidated, with its remaining population murdered in the forests on the city's outskirts, or deported to concentration camps.

Partly due to my age, being 12 at the time, and partly due to luck, I was not officially registered either in the ghetto or the labour camp. The danger of being discovered, however, was very real and it became necessary to find some hiding place for me. Fortunately, with my looks, I could pass for a Polish girl quite easily. I also had papers, under my mother's maiden name of Kulawicz, which was not a Jewish-sounding name, identifying me as a Catholic. My father and brother approached a number of their non-Jewish friends who were prepared to take me in, despite the danger to their own lives, should I be discovered. Living in a small community, people are naturally very inquisitive. The arrival of someone new into a household naturally raised suspicion. Who is that person? Is it your sister's child? Where did she come from? So I would stay with a family until people began to suspect something and when it became too dangerous I had to move on to the next family and the next.

Eventually, the time came when we ran out of families who were prepared to risk their own lives by providing me with a place to hide. At that time, together with several of his friends, my brother was building a hiding place in the forest surrounding our city. It was a bunker or, in fact, a reinforced hole dug into the earth and covered with branches and small trees. Faced with no alternatives, I had to move into the forest, into this bunker, where I lived for a number of months. It was a terrible situation, to be confined with perhaps ten other people in a very small space. For food, we were totally dependent on our friends, who would risk their lives with each trip from the city. During the day, we were not allowed to move out and it was only at night that we would go out to get some air, go to the toilet and do all the other things. Here, I existed from one day to the next, with the constant fear of being discovered at any moment.

After several weeks of hiding in the bunker, I didn't hear from my brother or father so I was getting very anxious. I didn't know at the time what happened to them. I later learnt that my brother was taken from our city to another labour camp where an airstrip was being built. He ran away from there, I think because he wanted to see that I was alright, and came back to Boryslaw, although I did not know this.

While still living in the bunker, I was sent a message by the head of the Jewish police, to go see him in the labour camp. He was the father of my brother's best friend and someone I loved very much. He had been on the first transport from our labour camp. Then, as head of the police, he was brought back by the Nazis, from Plaszow to Boryslaw, in order to calm the remaining Jews in preparation for the second deportation. So, I was taken to see him and spent several hours with him, in which he didn't say one word to me, he just took me in his arms, hugged me, cried and then arranged for the person who brought me, a non-Jewish person, to take me back to the forest. I asked him about my brother and he didn't answer me, asked for my father and didn't get any answer. So I went back to our bunker, which took several hours of walking, and there was nobody there. Not only our bunker, the whole forest was cleaned up. I will never know if he asked especially for me to come in order to save me, whether he knew the police were going to surround the forest and clear it of Jews.

I was then left standing in the forest with the guide who had taken me there, with the bunker empty and not knowing what to do next. After spending an agonising night in the forest, there was no alternative but to make the trek to the labour camp once again the next day in the hope of perhaps finding my father or brother there.

The guide took me as far as the outskirts of town, beyond that, the chance of being discovered was too great, and I went on alone from there to the labour camp itself. I knew that there was an entrance at the rear of the camp which was less guarded than the front one. I went there hoping to sneak in but as I got there so did the German police on horses and they started shouting at me, 'What are you doing here? You know you are not allowed to talk to Jews,' thinking that I wasn't one. So I quickly ran to the front entrance because I knew there were still the Jewish police there, that I'll recognise somebody there and they'll let me in. When I got there, I approached a Jewish guard, whom I knew, and asked to be let in and he said: 'Are you crazy? What are you doing here?' and I said, 'I want to come in' and he said, 'What for? You know what is happening?' I said I had to because I wanted to join my father and brother who I thought may be in the camp, and he said, 'Didn't you hear what happened yesterday?' He then told me that my brother, my father and my best friend were executed publicly the day before. That's how I found out. My brother attempted to run away again and was caught and, to set an example to all the others who remained, that that was what happens to Jews who attempted to run away, they were executed. I was in a state of complete shock. I said to myself, 'Well, I've got nothing to live for, I'm just going to go in,' and he said, 'No, I'm not going to let you in, go away,' and just as I was walking away I could see the German police arriving and surrounding the camp completely.

I then didn't have any idea what to do next, where to turn. I was trying to think of somewhere to turn, someone to turn to and I remembered a Polish friend of mine, whose parents were very decent people. But one has to remember that hiding a Jew was punishable by death, the danger was great and immediate. So I went over there and they were very nice to me, particularly the mother and her son, who was my friend. But the father was terrified of being caught. I had a shower there and the family allowed me to stay one night only and I left them in the morning. There was a little park nearby which had a few trees and a bench so I went and sat on the bench and said to myself, 'Well, what do I do now, where do I go?' And as I was sitting there I saw the whole transport being marched from the labour camp to the railway station surrounded by SS men, right before my eyes. That, I later learnt, was the last transport from our city, the Nazis having liquidated the labour camp, sending the Jews to Auschwitz. I sat there actually watching those people being marched by with all the police, all the dogs, and I even thought that someone would recognise me and say something. But so what. I mean, I didn't know what to do and, in any case, at that stage, I did not really care. But while I was sitting there, I thought of a place where a man I knew of was hiding a group of Jewish people. I decided to go there and to ask him to help me — there was nowhere else for me to go. He took me in and, 17 days later, the Russian troops liberated our town and that's how I survived. It was 1944 and I was 14 years old.

For the next couple of days, as word of liberation broke out, the survivors started emerging from their hiding places, heading for the main street, trying to find out who of their family had survived. I, of course, knew that no one from my family had survived; I was 14 and completely alone. As I wandered through the street, I saw the auntie of my brother's best friend. She, her daughter and the daughter's husband, had miraculously survived. When they learnt that I was left completely alone they immediately offered to take me into their home.

As incredible as it seems, life, in fact, did have to return to some semblance of normality and as part of that, I was to return to school. It is impossible to adequately describe what adjusting to this new life was like. I did not trust anyone, not my teachers, not those around me at school. But there was a certain zest for learning in me and I began concentrating on my studies.

A few years went by and in 1947, being a Polish citizen, I was faced with the option of remaining in what was now the Ukraine in the Soviet Union or to be repatriated in Poland. I did not wish to remain and decided to go to Poland, where I met my future husband and we married a year later. We did not wish to remain in Poland and we planned to emigrate to the United States. But the Polish quotas for the US were small and it was a very lengthy waiting list. A few friends of ours who emigrated to Australia wrote and told us how wonderful it was there and that it was a country which had opened up its doors. So in 1950, as I was expecting our first child, we emigrated to a safe haven, to Australia.

The immigrant's life is not an easy one. I spoke French, Polish, Russian and German but not English, so there was a period of adjustment for us. But we settled fairly quickly and my husband was very entrepreneurial, very capable. My daughter was born and very soon we led fairly normal lives. Once I had the language, it was, of course, easier.

Living in Australia, while I no longer hid my Jewish identity, as I had done just after the war, I was still not fully comfortable identifying as a Jew. In fact, I did not feel a part of any particular group and was not a member of any Jewish organisation or synagogue. Things changed, however, when my son's children were born. At that time, he came to me and during our conversation said, 'Well Mama, maybe it's time to make peace.' Largely because of his influence, I then joined the Reform temple in Sydney, originally doing this for him. But then I discovered that I felt very comfortable there, that I finally found a little corner where I could belong. And although I'm not a religious person — I'm now married to a non-Jew — I do celebrate Jewish holidays.

So, having found some peace, I often thought that there had to be a meaning to my survival and I felt a need to contribute. So how could I contribute? I tried, for instance, to work in the Jewish Museum as a guide but I found that I couldn't cope with that, it was too emotional. Then a dear friend of mine approached me and told me she was developing an oral history project for schools and asked if I would be prepared to talk to children about my experiences. At first, I was very hesitant because up until that time I had not spoken a lot about it. But I agreed and I actually found the experience to be a wonderful one, a cleansing experience in a way. Then I was asked whether I would like to join the Speaker Service of the Jewish Board of Deputies which gave me the opportunity to speak to non-Jewish school children, which I was pleased to do.

While giving these talks is very satisfying, it's also very difficult. And it doesn't get easier, no matter how many times I speak to groups. Each time I speak about the past I have to reconstruct it in my mind, in order to portray it to young people, so that they may understand what happened. I remember the past but I do not live in it. My concern is for the present and the future. I feel very strongly about prejudice and people who remain silent. It happened to me so often that I was in the company of non-Jews and they would say something derogatory about Jews and I would remain silent. I wouldn't say anything because I was too afraid. We have to speak up, we cannot remain silent.

I'm not an atheist. I believe in something larger than us, some cosmic consciousness. I can't believe it's all just an accident. And yet, when I think of the horrors that have happened, the way the children died, and I think is it just we're here and we go and that's the end of it? I don't know, I don't have a clear-cut answer. I have, for instance, a friend of mine who went to Auschwitz, she's an atheist, it's very clear-cut with her. But it's not with me. When I'm in trouble I pray to God, I suppose.

I try to explain my survival to myself, which of course I can't. But I think it is important to convey to people, especially young people, the injustices and hatreds of the past, and the present. And if in some way I have been able to affect some young people through relaying my experiences, then perhaps I have achieved something, perhaps my survival is serving a purpose. But I am also extremely grateful for my survival because since the horrors of the war life has been good to me. When people ask what my greatest achievement has been I tell about my children who have grown to become compassionate, caring and very decent people. There can be no greater achievement or reward in life.

Decorated War Veteran

Paul Cullen

Paul is a veteran of several campaigns who, as a Jewish soldier, gained the highest of decorations fighting for the Australian army. He founded the Reform movement in Sydney, despite his father and grandfather being presidents of the Great Synagogue. He is 88 years old, hard of hearing and experiencing eye problems, yet is spritely and articulate.

I was born in 1909. Cohen was my name. You know why we changed our name? During the campaign in Greece I was cut off because the German tanks broke through and came up behind us, and so I escaped. That's a long story of its own and well covered in other histories. I thought to myself, if I'm going to be taken prisoner by the Germans, Cohen is not a very good name to have. So I said to my brother, I think we ought to change our name, as so many in our family have already done, from Cohen to Cullen. So we went to the Australian Consul in Jerusalem and changed our name.

I was born in Newcastle. I don't remember much of that because we left when I was four. Family mythology, which is a bit different to family legend, which is a bit different to family history, says the reason we left Newcastle, which was a coal port, is that mother couldn't stand the washing getting covered in coal dust, and she said, 'I can't stand it any more.' But I think that my grandfather at that stage was getting elderly and he wanted my father, the oldest son, to come to Sydney and help him with the business.

Sir Samuel Cohen was my father. He was an eminent businessman of Sydney, Chairman of the Australian Gaslight Company and the Director of Tooth and Company, the biggest brewers of those days, and a number of other companies including our family company David Cohen and Co, of which he was the managing director.

My grandfather was a businessman and he was brilliant. When he died, at the age of 93, he was a genuine millionaire in pounds, which is quite different from being a millionaire today. Their house was the first private residence to have a lift in it. They had a parlour maid, a house maid, a cook, a kitchen maid, and a chauffeur, and my grandmother had a ladies' maid, a staff of seven.

Rumour has it my grandfather was offered a Knighthood but he declined it, and I'm prepared to believe that. It's also family mythology that the Duke of Edinburgh, when he was out here, wanted to go to my grandfather's wedding. My grandfather said, 'No, it's just curiosity and I'm not interested.'

My grandfather was born in Maitland and his father, Samuel Cohen, came to Australia in 1828. My maternal great-grandmother was the daughter of a convict.

My brother George is seven years older then me and when the war broke out, in 1939, I was 30 and he was 37, which is old to be a military soldier, and anyway he couldn't see well enough. So to get him to the army at all he got into the Army Service Corps, supply. He did a wonderful job as supply officer and he was awarded an MBE and I was awarded a DSO and the presentation was made at Government House on the same day. My father was justifiably proud that his two sons were being decorated on the same day. It was quite something really.

Tomorrow I'm being presented with a 60-year badge as a chartered accountant. If you live long enough everyone wants to present you with a badge. The honour I feel is the greatest is a difficult question. If you're talking protocol I'm a Companion of the Order of Australia, that's the equivalent of a Knighthood, which my father was also, Sir Samuel Cohen. I also got an AO, which is an Officer of the Order of Australia. Those are civil decorations. Then I've got military decorations: CBE, Commander of the British

Empire, that was pretty exciting, then I got two Distinguished Service Awards for gallantry in battle.

In 1927, I was called up in the militia. This was an idea for compulsory military training and everyone at 17 or 18 was called up and I went. And you can't say you've got a national service when you've got no one to train them, and the Australian regular army at that stage was tiny and we had half a dozen people to train thousands of conscripts, so it collapsed after a year. But I remained in the militia, I enjoyed it. I stayed in it and by the time the war broke out I was a captain.

I was married in 1932. She was a non-Jewish girl. At that stage I have to say my family were, and considered themselves, the premier Jewish family in Sydney, but apart from our own family I didn't meet many Jewish people. It was an extraordinary situation. Our whole circle of friends and acquaintances, people whose parties or weddings we went to, was just an extended family situation and that's why perhaps I was tempted to go out with non-Jewish girls. I think it's as typical thing, it happens all over the world, I'm not saying anything unusual.

My mother's house was not kosher. I don't think they had bacon or prawns, but they did not keep kosher. Her father was a very wealthy man and the land for a St Kilda synagogue was given by him, along with some money, to build the synagogue. But he wasn't an Orthodox Jew. My mother, having grown up in a non-Orthodox household, used to get impatient about Friday night prayers. I wouldn't have the faintest idea if she was agnostic or atheist or believed in Judaism, but she certainly never indicated any zeal for Judaism. My father tried to educate us, Mr Wolinski taught me for my bar mitzvah.

Then I got irritated with the dogmatic zeal of some of the rabbis and I said to my father, 'I think I will found a liberal Jewish synagogue,' that was 1937. So I founded the Temple Emanuel. I raised a lot of money for it because I had a sort of status through my family. My father, president of the Great Synagogue, defended me by saying 'Better half a Jew than no Jew.'

He was quite pleased really because he could see there was no use pretending. I just didn't have the zeal for Orthodox Judaism. What I liked about the idea of Liberal Judaism is that I don't speak Hebrew, I know some songs and hymns, but they didn't mean much to me, they were an impediment on my Jewish faith, on monotheism. I'm still a member of the congregation.

We had no trouble. It was a success from the start. Within a year we built a temple and we raised a lot of money for it. In those days, Jews weren't as rich as they are now. It wasn't an issue in the community. It never occurred to me that I was doing something heretical, if that's the word to use, and we never had any trouble getting people. In fact, we were surprised how many people wanted to join us.

I said to my children, who were born in 1932, 'You decide what you want to be, Jewish or non-Jewish.' I said, 'Don't tell me now, when I see you again, maybe next year, you can tell me what you want to be.' Because I went back to the war, to another campaign. They were brought up by my father in a quasi-Orthodox house while I was away and they went to Anglican schools, so they'd seen both sides. And when I came back, by that time I was Cullen, not Cohen, their names had been changed, and they decided that they wouldn't become Orthodox Jews.

Those were very disturbing times. Old standards were set aside, old standards are always set aside. The rabbis say unless you stick to old standards gradually everything will be swept aside, and that Liberal Judaism had not a word of Hebrew in it and you might as well call them Callithumpians, and I think the rabbis are probably right, I'm not saying the are wrong.

My father was not a Zionist. Sir Isaac Isaacs, who was the Governor-General, and his wife was a cousin of mine, so we used to mix in those circles too. He was not a Zionist and he was the intellectual leader of the Jewish community. The reason they weren't Zionists is that they couldn't see how, by planting a lot of Jews in Palestine, all we were going to do was create a war with the Arabs. I mean, what was the alternative course? There came to be no alternative in 1935. I think it's a wonderful idea as a practical matter to put all the survivors of the Holocaust there. There was nowhere else for them to go.

I was involved in all sorts of proposals for them. While I went to America and England in 1938, everyone was talking to me about would it be possible for them to go to the Kimberley and what did I think about them going to Uganda. My father, who was president of the Great Synagogue, called a meeting in his office of people from every synagogue, there were 30 people there, and I was made honorary secretary of the German Jewish Relief Fund.

When we got that cable when Hitler was up, just before *Kristalnacht* and all that, all the Jews who could were getting out of Germany, so we were raising money for what was originally the German Jewish Relief Fund which became The Australian Jewish Welfare Society. The London Committee said, 'Well, it's much more important for you to keep your money in Australia and get permits for Jews to go there, because we don't think that they can all go to Palestine.'

As far as I'm concerned, I'll do anything for the Jewish community. Whether through Austcare or the Refugee Council of Australia, I've got more permits for refugee Jews before the war and after the war than maybe anyone else. I suppose maybe Syd Einfeld, between the two of us we got a hell of a lot of permits.

I went to Israel on this trip in 1938 and I am not a Zionist but I am totally pro-Israel. The heroism of the Israeli soldiers and the tradition which every successful army has, I say successful army, is that the officers lead from the front. I've seen a lot of soldiers, a lot of battles, I've been in Tobruk, Greece, Crete, Syria and the Kokoda Track and other New Guinea campaigns where you have officers leading from the front when it's required, necessary and appropriate.

I can't concede to miracles. I'm afraid, although I revere Judaism, I'm fairly well an agnostic. I don't think it's miracles, I think it's courage and efficiency. I mean the individual Arab is prepared to commit suicide, but that's different from the Arab army facing the Israeli army. The Israelis will prevail as they did in every other war.

When I was away at the war, my partners kept paying me the whole of my share of the partnership profits throughout the war. I had a wonderful partner, non-Jewish, at J A L Gunn and Cohen, the chartered accountancy partnership I formed in 1934. He was a wonderful man because when I became honorary secretary for the Jewish Welfare Society, we had our office there and we had all these refugees coming in. I came back from the war and I couldn't settle down to a firm of accountants that had become tax experts. The taxation laws from then on until now, they're that thick and I couldn't study. I tried to study it but I was disturbed mentally and emotionally by the war and it took a stronger man than me to settle down and carry on the practice. My firm was the leading taxation firm in Sydney. I felt I couldn't play my part so in 1947 I retired. My father was getting old and I became managing director of David Cohen and Co.

The war had a traumatic effect on me. Six years in the Australian infantry destroyed my faith in the Almighty, or weakened it shall we say. It was disturbing and you can logically say there's no explanation, you either believe in God or you don't. There's been battle and torture and extermination and slavery and terrible things. But we're getting into an area of metaphysical belief which is very hard.

Because of the war, and all sorts of circumstances, my first marriage was on the way out. It's not the only case where people are away for six years, it's almost inevitable, human nature being what it is. My wife was a very attractive girl. We kept together until the children were married. But my wife and I weren't madly in love anymore. Nevertheless, we led a very pleasant life with our children. They've each got four children and I've got 14 great-grandchildren and we're a very happy family.

I'm very lucky insofar as my health is concerned. I've had open heart surgery, cancer and had an eye removed. I was the first person hit by a shell splinter in 1940 but apart from a great bruise on my bottom it didn't affect me. In Greece, a German tank fired some bullets and two of them went through the tunic pocket of my coat and clipped my lucky sovereign which my mother gave me. Not a drop of blood. I've been remarkably lucky and here I am. My one eye has been removed and now they're going to operate on the other one. When you've only got one eye you're more concerned naturally than if you have two good eyes.

I was president of the Royal Blind Society for a long time. I'm also very involved in badgering the PM and Minister for Defence how they're not properly defending Australia. I've been involved in various organisations to promote the defence of Australia, both regular and reserve.

At one stage, I was invited to enter the NSW Upper House and I regret, definitely regret, I didn't do that, because I think I might have been able to help a bit more that way, but I was busy commercially.

I married again very happily. My present marriage has been going for 23 years. We live on a farm and do all the work on 1,300 acres and it keeps me healthy. One of my great-grandsons, his family lives in France where his father works for an international company, so the little boy came up to the farm and he's mad on riding horses. Well, there was a bitterly cold wind up there, 2,000 feet high, and I said, 'Would you like to go for a ride, William?' and there I was three times, Saturday morning, Sunday morning and Sunday afternoon. It's nice to have a child share your enthusiasm.

A Scientific Approach

Ron Penny

I meet with Professor Penny at the Centre for Immunology, St Vincents Hospital, Sydney, where the door is clearly marked, 'Professor Penny, Director'. Despite a gruelling schedule of patients and responsibilities, he appears completely relaxed and, instructing that no calls be put through, begins speaking of his background, atheism and Jewish continuity.

My father had always wanted to leave Poland. Neither he nor my mother were educated beyond high school, but my father was an extraordinarily intelligent person, extremely well-read and particularly interested in world politics; so he knew even in 1934, around the time he got married, that Poland had no future for his family. It was not only what was happening next door in Germany but because he was fearful of the discrimination against Jews that existed in Poland and didn't want to bring his children up in that environment. He had the usual anti-Semitic experiences as a child and decided Poland was a place to leave.

He visited Palestine shortly after he was married and found that Palestine was too difficult a country for him to live in at that time. One reason it didn't suit him, I should add, is that he was an opera singer. He was offered a position in the Warsaw Opera if he changed to Catholicism, which he wouldn't do. So one of the problems he could see was that in Palestine there were no career opportunities for a singer. As he didn't obtain a visa to America he decided on Australia. We left Poland in 1938, by boat from Gdansk and via London, to Sydney.

I was born in Poland in 1936 and that's influenced my view of the world very differently from my brother's, who was born here after the war. As you get older you become more aware of the remarkable accident of history that my parents left when they did. Not one of my father's three brothers and not one of my mother's two brothers and three sisters, parents, or their families, survived. They were all killed in the camps and one brother who escaped to Russia died from typhus.

Settling in Australia was very difficult for them. My mother in particular had great difficulties with language, culture, absence of family and relative lack of finance. In Warsaw, by contrast, their life had been very sophisticated and urbane.

My father couldn't get any work as a singer. It was virtually at the outbreak of war. At first, he worked in Paddy's market and then, over time, built up a successful men's clothing business. He actually made quite a good living out of it, with considerable help from my mother.

Once the war broke out, we had letters coming from Europe and Russia. The last letter came in 1941. It was a desperate time for them, knowing what had gone on in Poland. It was only after the war, when they were able to go to the displaced persons' registry and find out, that we knew none of them had survived. Its impact on my parents was very profound, that there was no one left from probably a family of some 50 first-degree relatives.

That was a most depressing time. I was too young then to fully sense it, but I grew up aware deeply, and increasingly more so as time went by, of the Holocaust's impact. But my parents would never talk to me about it. That's a theme you've probably heard about repeatedly, and I still consider it tragic that my father, even until he died, never discussed a lot of the issues he thought and felt about. As his children, we've been denied that information and I'm obviously unhappy that I know so little about what he went through emotionally.

In Poland my parents were not highly observant. Certainly, they observed the High Holidays, but they were not deeply religious. In Sydney, after our arrival, we went to the Reform synagogue because that was more consistent with my parents' views but also because my father sang in the choir and we then became members. I had my bar mitzvah in the Temple. In fact, at eight years of age, for a short while, I wanted to be a rabbi! I went every afternoon to *cheder* and I enjoyed it. Although not highly observant, we certainly were committed Jews and both my brother and I were brought up with strong Jewish values.

As you go through life, you change your thinking about religion. When I studied science at high school, in the early 1950s, and started to read about some of the prevailing theories of the universe from Einstein, Eddington and Hoyle, I remember having numerous debates with my father about the existence of God, and I became and remain an atheist. And even though I am very Jewish, I have a problem with theology.

Those lengthy debates with my father explored the origins of the universe, the basis of theology and the conflict between science and religion, which I've always resolved in my mind on a scientific basis. I don't see theology serving any purpose other than as social and personal value. But as for providing an intellectual explanation for the origin or order of the universe, I don't accept it.

Studying the universe, the more I read about the creation of the universe — and this is going back to the late 40s and early 50s when astronomy was not well developed — the science of it was so fascinating to me that there wasn't room in that theory for a supernatural being to create the universe. It didn't fit into the way I thought about science and still doesn't.

I can recall convening one of the State Zionist Council seminars, which must have been 15 years ago or so, and there was a discussion panel titled 'Who is a Jew?' We had a whole range of people, from Orthodox and Conservative rabbis, sociologists and so on. The answer that most appeals to me now is that a person is a Jew who calls himself a Jew. There is perhaps no other way you can really define it, to be all-encompassing, to account for the Zionists and non-Zionists, religious and irreligious, Reform, and people with views like myself. I'm religious in the sense that I am partially observant, I'm culturally strong in my Jewish identity, on Jewish history and I want my children and their children to be brought up Jewish. I believe in the Jewish way of life but the theosophical component I don't hold. I'm quite comfortable being a culturally identifying Jew and at the same time not believing in God. Some people may find that position unacceptable.

I have a respect for those who believe but I don't believe. Unless you can prove a belief on scientific grounds, you then have a fundamental hypothesis that either God created or God didn't create the universe. I don't believe God created the world.

I'm not judgemental on belief systems and I don't expect other Jews to hold my views. To me, however, there is value in Orthodoxy. They are the curators of the Jewish faith and Jewish traditions. They are the preservers of a culture and a belief system which have served well for centuries. It's different when the Orthodox dictate to the rest of the Jewish people. That's when conflicts arise, as now in Israel, where they impose what I consider unacceptable constraints on other Jews.

If you ask me what the motivation for my Jewish identity is, part of the motivation is respect for my forefathers and foremothers, because they died for their Jewish identity. So it's hard for me to reject it. I fear subsequent generations will feel differently.

One important element in my life has been the Jewish tradition of learning. If you were religious, you studied the Torah and if you were not religious you still studied, and study as a goal in itself is actually an important Jewish ideal. The encouragement of learning, and the pursuit of higher qualifications, has been a very strong impetus for Jews.

I'm a big believer in mentors: people who directly influence you during your life, usually as teachers. Others may not even know of the impact they have. A science teacher in Sydney High was my most significant mentor who really stimulated me, not just in learning but inquiring and exploring deeply into the world around me.

Our Jewish community is a very successful one, compared with communities I've seen elsewhere. Although it's small, its vibrant approach to issues like Jewish education has intensified remarkably over the past few decades. That really is a very strong force in the community and is also its salvation. Continuity depends on the young coming through this education system. To assist this process, there have been a number of very successful leaders in the community. The community, fortunately, has also been successful financially, which has allowed it to generate resources that have fed back to those in need, here and in Israel.

Also, I think the Jewish community is more mature now than it used to be. When I lived in America in the 60s, Jews always talked openly about being Jewish. When there was a Jewish holiday it would be announced on the radio in New York and they'd suspend parking restrictions in the city, and everyone knew it. Here, it's taken until the last few years for the Jewish community to become outspoken on Jewish issues. People in the mainstream media will now talk about Jewish holidays and other Jewish issues freely. The hesitancy that the Australian Jewish community used to have about speaking out has been fortunately overcome.

The area that the Jewish community has not nurtured is the encouragement, development and support of young Jews into high-profile positions in politics, political science, government and the media. I believe, as in other walks of life, we need input into the decision-making policies of our democracy.

I'm less involved in the community now than I used to be. I was once very active. I was for a number of years head of the Jewish doctors' group and worked with the *UIA* but, regretfully, the pressures of work commitments have become all-consuming.

My work day runs from 7.00am to 7.00pm most days a week with considerable night and weekend activities, and there are many commitments in many areas so I'm always juggling time. The main priority is my family, with whom I spend most of my time outside work. We now have four grandchildren from our two children and their spouses and still three in the generation ahead of us, currently my mother is living happily in the Montefiore home. I also have a great love of classical music, which for me is spiritual nourishment, intensely personal, and enormously enriching.

Reflections on a Life of Orthodoxy

Melita Stillchweig

Frail and sometimes forgetful, Melita, just two years away from celebrating her centenary, lives in the nursing unit of the Montefiore Home, a Jewish home for the aged. I am introduced to her by her great- granddaughter, who is in her late 20s. Our arrival interrupts a visit from Melita's friend on the next floor and similarly we are interrupted throughout the interview by visitors, companions, nursing staff and cleaners. On her bedside table sits a Jewish prayer book and on the wall a plaque thanking her for dedicated work with the home's synagogue. In a thick German accent she speaks from her bed about her early life in Germany and 98 years of commitment to Orthodox Judaism.

(I have interspersed this interview with another [in italics], conducted by her great-grandson several years earlier.)

MELITA: I come from Germany, from Giessen in Hessen.

Giesen in Hessen was originally a fortress; the castle in the middle of town was surrounded by beautiful gardens. My father built our first house in the West Avenue, it consisted of three storeys, a garden in front and a large courtyard in the back.

The Kaiser came every year. It was a great event with a holiday for the whole city. Our Archduke also came on that occasion and once, shortly before the First World War, Tzar Nicholas joined in. I can still see these three men driving through the streets sitting in an open carriage.

We had a very good life and a very religious life, very *frum*. We were six children. There is a picture on the shelf, you can see my parents and the children. Behind there is my little brother, he later trained dogs in Israel. He was very sick, fought in the Israeli war, and died very young. My sister over there was like my mother to me because my parents had six children, eight actually, but two passed away very early.

My father was a judge of the Arbitration Court for produce merchants and greatly respected. He was a wealthy man but money was never mentioned in our house. We all had music lessons and our dresses and all the boys' suits were bought in Frankfurt where there was a special children's shop. I remember that once my mother had some hats made for my sister and myself out of black taffeta and with white lace ruffles inside the brim. I thought it was the most beautiful and elegant hat ever.

We were snobs in our own way, which I didn't realise at the time. My parents' friends were our rabbi, doctor and business associates. We didn't mix with the shop keepers and only visited them on special occasions. Today, I look back and I would like to know what they thought of us, if there was a feeling of envy or disdain.

My parents seemed rather remote and removed from us and I can only remember a dutiful good-night kiss but never any display of affection.

MELITA: My mother was a very clever woman, very knowledgeable. My mother learnt with the boys, she was full of knowledge. I must say my mother knew much more than I ever learnt.

My father had a good education but my mother's knowledge was outstanding. She had learned French and English, played the piano, had a tremendous Jewish knowledge.

My father with some of his contemporaries founded our first synagogue. Later, my father was elected president of the second synagogue and a member of many organisations.

From an early age my mother made me accompany her to the hospitals visiting the sick and delivering kosher food. Later, I was sent visiting families and taking food parcels to them. We always had strangers at our table whom father brought home from synagogue.

MELITA: I was visiting my sister who worked in Berlin when I met my husband. He fell in love with me. I was at the time in university studying chemistry and physics because I was very eager to go on. I took a bit of Latin also, but only a little bit because it was too much for me. I had strong ambitions. I wanted to go on. And then I met my husband and I put everything down and I married. University just wasn't so important anymore. That is foolish.

The reason we left Germany was because of Hitler, that is the reason why the Jews left, the Holocaust. In Germany the Jews couldn't live anymore where there was Hitler; the people were sent to concentration camps and were killed. Therefore, we wrote to Australia for our permit and we got it because we told our life story: who we are and what we do and we got the permit to come to Australia. We were lucky. We came here and my parents went to South Africa because another sister lived already in South Africa.

We came to Australia by boat, from Europe. It was *Channukah* and we lit candles for eight days. I remember people came onto our cabin and we sat together and kindled the lights.

We arrived here in 1939. We didn't know anyone, I don't think we had anyone to meet us. I couldn't tell you how we settled anymore. We must have had some English otherwise it wouldn't have been possible. Perhaps I knew a bit of English anyway because of school and so on. But one forgets. It's amazing when you think back — to start with nothing at all.

We got to Australia and that was marvellous. We probably then started making dresses because that's what my husband knew. Yes, that's right, my husband started a ladies' clothes factory because that was not known here then, everything was ordered from overseas. And we started making dresses and so dressmaking came to Australia. I'm surprised I can remember all this because I am old, I am nearly 100. My mind is not so bad, considering the age, and still remembering. Then we had a factory with 70 workers.

My husband doesn't live any more, he was a very sick man. He was a very good person. He died very early. I then had to work, not in the factory, in a shop, a dry-cleaning shop. One day he said to me I shouldn't leave him alone anymore and three days later he died.

That was the end and I continued with the Tip Top dry cleaning, I had to earn money. One can do so much if one has to.

I had two daughters, one has passed away unfortunately, the younger one. She passed so very early, comparatively early. It was too much. She was in the factory working, cutting, sewing, making dresses and she stopped. The other daughter is in England. She has a very fine man who is a Professor of Mathematics and he just retired. He's 83 and she is 73 years old and they live in England, Cambridge. She is very clever, she also paints very well.

I used to go to synagogue every week. I don't go so much now, on a *Shabbat* morning. But I always have my prayer books here. Every night I wouldn't go to sleep without saying my Hebrew prayers. One learns, one knows it, one does it. I am a Jewish woman. I cannot walk so much now, I have trouble with my legs. It's too much sitting and waiting. Everyone should live according to themselves, some people love going to synagogue and other people do not like to go. Everyone should live as they think is right. But Jewish for me is always, there is nothing missing in Jewishness. Religion was always there. From the beginning to the end.

Religion in our home was taken for granted. A Shabbos *was a* Shabbos, *a day of rest, a* Yom Tov *was a* Yom Tov, *everything done with strict observance. We had private religious lessons apart from Scripture lessons at school and Sunday morning teaching.*

You can't imagine how much cleaning went on before Pesach. *Every dish and saucepan was scraped and cleaned before putting away. Silver was boiled, glass stood for three days in water. We didn't feel it as restriction or an unpleasant duty. It was all a matter of course.*

MELITA: This here is a good place, excellent, a Jewish home. Everything is completely kosher, everything is Jewish. See that certificate the wall, that is for me, I did a lot of things with the synagogue here. I had many more certificates, they were hanging in another room, not here. I am now an old woman, I am 98 years old and when I was younger I was very active to learn and to organise, I was in women's organisations, doing things, but one gets older and older and it isn't easy for me any more as it used to be when I started.

When I look back, I think I was a good woman because I knew quite a lot and I could help other people. We had *B'nai B'rith* and Jewish Women's Organisations and I was in them from the beginning and I was always religious. I only know that I was always connected with religion.

Spiritual Healing

Kitty Finger

Kitty's business card describes her as promoting healing and holistic wellbeing through bio-energy polarity. We sit in her living room, surrounded by photos of her grandchildren and within sight of her work area, once the kids' rumpus room, where she teaches yoga and offers counselling.

I really don't reflect on the Holocaust unless I'm asked. My husband, for instance, he was in concentration camps and dwells much more on that side of things. Don't forget, although I had the experience of being separated from my parents and evacuated and the Blitz and bombing, it still wasn't a concentration camp experience, which is a totally different ball game.

I was born in Vienna and left when I was six on a children's transport that went to England. My mother came six months later. My father was supposed to join us, but it was too late. He was sent to Auschwitz.

My mother and I came to Australia when I was 16. I worked in hairdressing and it happened to be the establishment where I met the person who later became my husband. Even though we didn't have very much financially, when our children were born, because I had the background of not living with my mother as a child, and having lost my father during the war, I was determined to be a full-time mother in their pre-school years.

When they started school I went for a short while into my husband's business, which was clothing manufacturing, but I recognised very early on that the business world was not for me. Through a series of circumstances, which the *Celestine Prophecies* calls synchronicity, I was led into teachers' training for yoga teaching. Yoga involves the holistic principles of physical, mental and spiritual wellbeing. It's an outlook on life. A total philosophy.

Conducting yoga classes, I naturally became involved in the day-to-day problems of my students, and often found myself in the role of counsellor. I then decided to do a formal diploma course in psychotherapy counselling which made it possible for me to combine this function with my other qualified teachings.

When people come to me to discuss a problem I do this in the relaxed comfortable atmosphere of my study and make the situation as informal as possible. I chat with them and use my intuitive sense to a degree and really listen to what they have to say.

Once a person is able to talk freely to someone outside their situation it not only relieves the pressures but helps to sort things out in their mind. I have often sat for an hour listening, and saying very little, and the person says 'Thank you, you've been a great help, because you've listened.'

Intuitiveness, being tuned into the self and universal consciousness, is to me most important, and is the basis of all my studies, teachings and therapies. Especially in bio-energy polarity, healing and therapeutic touch, with which I am very much involved through the Holistic Nurses Association. These therapies depend greatly on inner-guidance when giving a treatment. Often at such a time my hands seem to take on a life of their own. I don't want to say too much about this as not everyone relates to these concepts as yet.

The word religion to me is a total misnomer. We were brought up on such conditioning as — 'If you're not a good person God will punish you.' As a thinking person I could not accept a God sitting on high in judgement. God, as I understand it, is neither good nor evil, but one power, a presence — an omnipotence, and this presence, or God consciousness, is within us.

While I was going through this transition my husband thought I was moving away from Judaism, and blamed my yoga teachings and wanted me to give up my work in this direction. But after much battling he began to accept my ideas, although his views on religion did not change.

Being Jewish, of course we have strong roots and I'm very much aware of them. We, as a family, are traditionally observant of *Rosh Hashana* and *Kippur, Pesach* et cetera. But I don't follow these festivals out of superstition or because I've been told that's what I have to do. We also observe the Sabbath to the degree of lighting candles, having *challah* and wine on the table, so that the grandchildren are aware of their Jewish heritage also.

Tradition and Jewishness are important to me, but I am not as caught up by it as my husband who still keeps the older view of religion and Judaism. For instance, I don't think I would have been as devastated as he would have been if our children had chosen to marry non-Jewish people. As long as they were good human beings and would make my children happy.

As I've said, I'm very aware and proud of my Jewish background. I'm not in favour, however, of members of the Orthodox community going on the street wearing *talitim* or *shtreimels,* and certainly not happy about them asking strangers on the street 'Are you Jewish?' at festival times. I feel as a people we already have enough problems without attracting more attention and demonstrating our cultural differences in a country where we are in the minority and which is for many of us an adoptive country.

I suppose you could say I try to follow a spiritual path rather than a religious one, and there is a difference. The Torah has got some wonderful teachings but studying it or attending synagogue regularly does not make one either religious or spiritual in the true sense.

Religion and spirituality to me is primarily to strive and be a worthwhile human being who cares about others regardless of nation, colour or creed. And when people speak of the coming of the Messiah, whose form seems very nebulous to me, I feel that if we become more loving and caring about each other and be our brother's keeper we would enter a messianic age.

I never hide the fact that I'm Jewish, on the contrary, whenever I acquire a new student I make my origins known. In all my dealings, with a cross-section of the community, I've never encountered any problems in this regard. And I'm very happy that my grandchildren go to a moderate-oriented Jewish school and that they are aware of their Jewish background and know where they are from. And this will hopefully help them to know where they want to go in life.

I'm a very independent person. I can go with the flow, but I can't go with the flock. That makes it sometimes difficult for my family and friends to understand me and the activities I enjoy. But that's all right as I don't always understand them and their pastimes either. But the important thing is that everyone enjoys their chosen recreations and activities. I feel fortunate to have found a path that is satisfactory to me.

I also am very fortunate and appreciative of the fact that my children have caused me no major problems and like to think I haven't given them too many either. I also enjoy my wonderful in-law children and we all enjoy a good family relationship.

I hope to go on learning and teaching forever. What else would I do? What would I retire from and to? I love what I do, I have enough to keep me continuously interested. I enjoy studying various principles, especially in regard to holistic health and wellbeing. What I do need is a few more lifetimes for all that I'd still like to achieve. So I'm hoping I get some reincarnations along the way.

Defeating the Odds

Sarolta Budai

Sarolta welcomes me to her home with a broad smile which radiates genuine warmth. Her upbeat and jovial manner effectively disguises the horrifying experiences of her past. Despite having lived through several concentration camps and later having her husband imprisoned for many months by the communists, her eyes do not project the sadness I expected. Rather, she is cheerful, beaming and, at over 70, exuding energy. She joins her son Tommy and me at the dining room table.

Tommy was born in Australia, in the Royal Hospital. What went wrong I do not really truly know. One day his head got blood that went in and didn't dissolve completely — a blood clot, which made him how he is. He's not bad, in some ways he is even better than he should be.

He was born with two cataracts and, when he was five, I had advice to have it removed and unfortunately, because we don't speak English well enough, we listened to this and listened to that. I made my biggest mistake and made an operation on his eye which unfortunately he lost. He's still got a cataract on the other eye which nobody will touch. He's got used to it, he's got to have drops every day.

I had one doctor when he was 18 months old, who said to me: 'Make him believe he's just like everybody else and slowly he will catch up. Make him believe he can mix with people because he's no different.' The doctor's advice was let him do everything he could, and we let him do it. And now he's got — I don't know how you say it — no fear. He's got no problems with people.

When he was only in kindergarten we had a little shop opposite the park. My eldest son Frank said to me, 'Mum, let him go alone.' And the first time we ever let him go in the bus, Frank said, 'You're looking at him in pink glasses, let him go.' So I let him go and that's how he got how he is. I just let him go and let him do. So he lives a full life.

He started school in Tempe which was my biggest luck. It was a small school with disabled and troubled children and the headmaster said, 'If they are being pushed they can do things and learn' and that's how he can read and write.

When he was 18 years old and school was finished, I thought, what should I do with him now, put him in a workshop? I knew if I put him in a workshop he would go backwards. Luckily, we had a shop in town and the manager said, 'No, we won't let Tommy go to the workshop, we're going to use him here.' That's how he got into working with people because he does everything for anyone who wants anything. He can do banking, he can do everything — alterations, and stuff like that. In time, we closed our shop and my eldest son's wife knew the man who would become Tommy's boss, at the law firm. They took him in just to try and he's been working there since then.

I'm very happy because if he didn't have this job what would he do? People love him. Ask around town! Everybody knows Tom and everybody likes him. I can't tell you why but he's always happy. Mind you, he's got a good life. Now there's only two of us, before, with my husband, who was also an easy-going person. He was, unfortunately, sick for many years. We travel a bit, quite a bit I should say. How many young men can say, 'I've been in Fiji, in Honolulu, I've been in Israel. Here and there.'

With his girlfriend Roxanne, it's a bit complicated. We talked about it not long ago. I was in *Hakoah* Club, we're talking around the table, and my friend says, 'Sarolta, what are you thinking, you're not getting any younger, you might have to let him go.' She said to me, 'Why don't you get a small unit and have them to sort their life?' And I said, 'I don't think so.' First of all I'm a bit greedy that way, I miss him when he's not home. Still, I let him to live his own life. I said, 'Tom, come here, I have something I want to ask you,' because we talk about everything. I said, 'How would you like to move out and to move with Roxanne?' and he said, 'No, not yet' and I said, 'What do you mean not yet, you're 40 years old, what are you waiting for?' and he said, 'No, not yet.' And then I asked him the other question, 'Would Roxanne like to move in here?' 'Oh yeah,' he said, 'That would be good.' But I thought about it and I said, 'Look, you can leave and I will help you all I can.' The house is already under his name, my two other boys don't need it so it's obvious when my husband got really sick we needed to do something, so we got his boss at the law firm over and put the house in Tom's name and made him guardian, trustee — 'One day this house will be yours and everything in it, but while I'm alive nobody else can live here'. Fair enough? I said, 'If you need help, if you want to move out, I'd be quite happy to help you but in here, I'm not going to clean up after any young woman.'

He knows what he wants. If he wants to come with me when I go away, he's welcome to it. We quite enjoy each other's company. I can't say much about the future. Who knows who is going first? He can manage his life, plus he's got a lot of friends. I know I have no problem because he can look after himself. He is maniacally clean so there are no problems in that area. And everybody is ready to help him if he needs it.

Two years ago, my 70th birthday was coming up and my granddaughter was in Israel and my eldest son came on Sunday morning and said 'I'm sending you to Israel to visit Angela.' So of course I told Tommy 'You have your money, you can save it, if you have enough you can come with me.' So we went to Hungary, we went to Israel. We were in Israel for about five weeks. We had a marvellous time. Absolutely.

Tommy knows he is Jewish. We go to *shul* on *Rosh Hashana, Yom Kippur.* Also, he loved Israel. But when we went to Israel we went to Yad Vashem and Tommy didn't like it, he had to get out, he couldn't stand it. He was crying and it was too much for him.

We were just chatting on Sunday with one of my friends. One of my friends, her job in Auschwitz was shaving the heads of people and

49

she is alive because of that, and one of my friends said, 'Tell that to that idiot man, the one who is saying it isn't happened, Irving, tell that to David Irving.' Because all of us sitting there, we all went through the camps in one way or another.

You can't make it go away. You sit down and cry to yourself but what's the use. My mother always told me there's always a corner where you can cry. Don't cry in front of other people.

I was in a concentration camp during the war. Everybody from my family died in there except myself and my sister. But we didn't make our children feel what we've been though, because it's no good. It wouldn't do any good. We just take it as it is. Sometimes it comes up. I had a sister-in-law who actually worked in the gas chambers and she doesn't talk about it.

I come back from the dead. What can I do? We arrived in Auschwitz and it was like, when we got of the wagon, we decided with my sister that we would keep my mum in between us and one of us would stay with her. But there was no chance because she had been selected and the Polish girls were screaming, 'Good on you, you're going to die in here.'

One year! For one year I worked with Mengele! And every minute when he turned around it could have been my last. I worked in an ambulance cleaning a lot of dead people, sick people and he came every day to select people and I could be selected every day. I was there in Auschwitz, two months in Bergen Belsen or something like that and we went to work in a factory and we got freed when my sister and I were in Terezinstaat.

Then we went back to Hungary because my sister thought she had a fiancé there. Unfortunately he wasn't there. Our family was all gone, we had nothing, and we lived back there. And you start your bloody life all over again and the people on the street in Hungary said, 'They said you're all dead and yet there are still more coming back.' The city I was in had 18,000 Jews in it and only 2,000 come back and they said too much come back.

Unfortunately, my sister died 23 years ago in a car accident. That was terrible. That was the biggest loss in my life because if she had not been with me I would never have survived. That was my biggest loss, my sister dying.

My husband was about to go to Israel in a group when I met him. We got married after three weeks of knowing each other and it was 48 years of a wonderful marriage. Then it wasn't finished, it's never ending. We were supposed to go to Israel. I had a little baby and we sold everything we had because on December 15 we would leave. On the 12th of December the government said we couldn't go anymore. So we started all over again. Then they put my husband in jail. Eighteen months he spent in jail, for nothing. They apologised when they let him out, 'It was a mistake.'

The first two boys were born in Hungary. We actually had a Jewish name then, Weis, but my eldest one was studying, and there was trouble in the school for children with Jewish names. My husband went to ask what was wrong and they said, 'He is too much in the end of the ABC' which, of course, was not true. And my husband said, 'All right, tell me what you want,' and in that time there were soccer players, two Budai boys, and so he chose them and that became our name.

In 1956 the revolution came and we left everything, I mean everything. Not even a change of clothes. We got the two children and we left. He said to me he's going to Australia, he's got no one nowhere but he wants to go as far as possible from the communism and so we came as far as possible.

When we arrived here we had no one and they sent us to Brisbane. The first thing after we arrived, after I don't know how many hours of travelling on the cold train, the person who was expecting us from the Jewish community at the train station said, 'Mr Budai did you bring some money?' and my husband said, 'Yes, 10 shillings.' We knew we couldn't stay there and because we had such a good friend in Sydney we got a letter to say we could find a job there. So my husband came first and found himself a job as a tailor. He couldn't speak a word of English. They told him, 'The machine doesn't talk, sit down and do what you do.' Then I came over with the two children. I was pregnant.

I tell you, my husband was always cheerful and looking to the best. There were plenty of Hungarians already here but to everyone who was coming, those who had been here a long time, said, 'Well, we started out poor too.' I had a friend who had a sister here who was quite well off, she said to me, 'I started like you, poor.' Then we found out life was getting really nice for us and were very, very happy. We always worked, didn't matter what work it was. We were lucky that our shop was really a little gold mine. We had a factory behind it, it was in leather clothing and that time it was fantastic. So it was quite all right. So we bought a unit up here. Two or three years later my husband got sick and eventually was paralysed.

I tell you, there is nowhere in the world like Australia. To start at that time, in 1957, with absolutely nothing — we had 10 shillings, two children and a third on the way — and with our two hands, we make it.

The Communal Leader

Diane Shteinman

With a life-long history of involvement in Jewish communal life through active participation in many organisations, Diane is currently president of the Executive Council of Australian Jewry — the roof body of the community. Significantly, she is also the organisation's first woman president. We meet in a small room in a building housing many of the community's offices.

When I was growing up in Melbourne, my father was very adamant that we were traditional, not so Orthodox, but very traditional. We lit candles on Friday night but then my father went out to play cards and I was allowed to do things on Friday night if I wanted to. As in my own life, being Jewish revolved around friends and family. My dad was very heavily involved in the Jewish National Fund, United Israel Appeal and also the setting up of a Jewish centre and synagogue in Kew. After the war many Jews moved away to other areas. My family went to live in Carlton which is on the other side of town from where most of the Jews lived — St Kilda and Caulfield.

My own communal life probably started when I was a teenager and the community centre was set up in our neighbourhood. We formed the Jewish younger set and I was involved in that. I felt pretty isolated in my teenage years because of living on the other side of town and having the long tram rides. When I was 12 or 13 I decided on my own volition to go the *cheder* at Toorak Synagogue which meant an hour and a half each way by public transport every Sunday. But I really enjoyed it.

When I got to university I became the secretary of the Jewish Students Society. Isi Leibler came up to me and said, 'We Zionists have to get rid of the communists on the Jewish students committee.' I remember it so clearly, it sounded so exciting and conspiratorial.

Isi, of course, went on to serve three terms as president of the Executive Council of Australian Jewry (ECAJ) and is now the chairman of the Governing Board of the World Jewish Congress and I'm now the president of the Executive Council of Australian Jewry.

When I finished physiotherapy we had something called the Melbourne Jewish Youth Council of which I remember being secretary. There was an office in the City and I hung around there a lot. It was a very exciting time. I became a rabid Zionist and promised myself I was going on *aliyah* and I even wrote a manifesto which I found recently, saying I definitely thought Israel was the place to be and that's where I wanted to live but that I would also work for education in the Diaspora. I even talked about Jewish continuity and how important education was to continuity. The things that we think are current I was thinking about back then. When I finished studying, my father said he'd pay for a ticket for me to go to Israel on the condition that I came back at the end of the year for my brother's bar mitzvah. So of course I grabbed that and went and had a wonderful year, worked as a physiotherapist and decided, yes, that's where I wanted to live. But I kept my promise to come home and was planning to go back.

At home I worked as a physiotherapist and became involved in a few fund-raising organisations like Friends of Hebrew University and Young United Israel Appeal, and the following year I met Bob Shteinman who said that he'd spent a year in Israel and was planning to go back too. I thought it was terrific and I was in love with him anyway. So I thought we'll get married and go to Sydney which I was very happy about. We came to live in Sydney and it took me about 20 years to finally realise I wasn't going on *aliyah*.

It was probably not until my eldest son, David, went to kindergarten that I became involved in communal life in Sydney. I joined the committee and we started talking about a Jewish day school, which eventuated in 1966 when we opened Masada College.

This really took up just about all my waking hours. We did everything. It wasn't easy to convince people to send their child to a Jewish day school. People just got sick of the sight of us I think. We badgered them. Bob and I used to arrive at dinner parties and people would say don't talk about Jewish day schools. But we did, and we also had to raise the money and work very hard.

When a number of people said they didn't drive so how would their child get to school I became the transport officer and I drove kids in my station wagon for quite a few years and then I hired ladies with station wagons. Now they have a fleet of buses. But that was well after my time.

I more or less finished with Masada when my youngest daughter, Ruth, finished her primary school. That's when I started to get involved in Wizo which I enjoyed very much because you were dealing with a very large membership all around Australia so you had the possibility of reaching thousands of women.

Wizo was good. It was the time when, for example, they were thinking of setting up a PLO office in Canberra and it was something that at the time we were against. We did it within days. We sent out messages and the letters came pouring in to the government in Canberra, so much so that the Israeli ambassador was able to tell us it was really Wizo that had made the difference.

That was also where I first became involved in the Soviet Jewry campaign — the other great event of my life I suppose. Somebody suggested that we send a message to Ida Nudel who was then in exile and I was given the job to organise it. So I wrote to a group in London and that started a correspondence and my interest and involvement really took off. Bob was really interested because he belonged to a group that had always been trying to do something about Soviet Jewry but it had been hushed by a policy of softly, softly. Isi Leibler turned all that around with his activity. He was the one who originally went to the Australian government and they were the first to bring it up in the United Nations. So a lot happened in Australia.

I then came to the Board of Deputies as a Wizo representative and joined the Oppressed Jewry Committee. I used to borrow the files and read them avidly and started to make contact with all the groups that were active around the world. Then in 1985 I went to Jerusalem to the World Jewish Congress assembly and met all the people who were involved in the issue.

One of the highlights was when we sent a petition around to all the parliamentarians asking for Soviet Jews to be released and then we went to Canberra and took the petition to the Soviet embassy, together with members of the three main political parties, and they refused to accept the petition. We immediately went back to the Senate which was sitting that afternoon and whoever was with us from the Senate said 'Mr President, we've been to the Soviet embassy and they refused to accept a petition of this Australian parliament' and then all the assembled senators whose names hadn't been on the petition jumped up saying 'I want my name associated with that too.' So we were really the flavour of the month and we got onto television that night.

I continued as Oppressed Jewry consultant to the ECAJ and was getting interested in being involved in across-the-board activities. I then became secretary of the Board of Deputies and was offered to be president and declined and said I'd rather have the other job — the one I'm doing now, nationally.

The big issue facing the community, everyone will tell you, is continuity. I'm really proud of the Australian Jewish community. I think it's really an excellent community and especially in comparison to other Diaspora communities. We now have almost a 40-year history of Jewish day schools, which must make a difference to our continuity. I'm not saying it's the answer and it's perfect but it must make a difference. I think our relationship with Israel is strong in the numbers that have gone on *aliyah*, it's like ten per cent of the Australian community. And the number of Jews who travel to Israel from Australia — I think 45 per cent of the community has been to Israel. I don't believe we're going down the American path where there is 50 or 60 per cent intermarriage. Which doesn't mean we sit back and take it easy, we've got to concentrate on what we're going to do. Nobody seems to have the answer. I guess if we keep talking about it that's something. I've always been very concerned with young adults and at the ECAJ we really are trying to see if we can somehow stimulate activity in that sphere or at least to just monitor it or find out what's happening.

Sometimes we think we aren't a very cohesive community and then when we look at other communities we realise we are. There don't seem to be too many contentious issues. We seem to be able to engender, for example, support for Israel, regardless of whatever government is in power, whatever government is democratically elected in Israel. Everybody, of course, has their views but it doesn't seem to create divisiveness in the community as I think it did in the past, when I was growing up.

With Reform and Orthodox there seems to be, particularly in Sydney, a certain amount of respect between the two. We've learnt how to cope with the sort of anomalies and sometimes quite ridiculous strictures that do exist. In order not to create crises we skirt around them, so we don't really face the issue but those issues certainly are there. If only they would come together on some ideas like conversion, there would be fewer problems.

The other issue is how to spend the communal fund-raising dollar. That's become a very divisive and contentious issue: whether more or less money should go to Israel or to the local community. Both really need the money. My predecessor created a huge furore when he said that because the Jewish schools were pricing out the middle class, that the United Israel Appeal should put some of their money into it, which just created such antagonism and really was counter-productive and did nothing whatsoever except create problems. That's not the way to go about it.

As a woman I have never had any restrictions or problems. I've just gone ahead and done whatever I wanted to. It's my contention that you should just get in there and do the work, which is how I started with every organisation. I didn't start in any organisation as the president or the member of the executive or anything, I just started out there like in Masada driving the children, baking the cakes, doing the ringing and whatever had to be done. And you get on a committee and if you show that you work you just move upwards. Unfortunately, a lot of the younger women seem to think they are prevented from doing various things or becoming leaders but you don't become a leader first, you have to prove yourself. Whatever I've done I've always done with a passion for the actual cause that I've been working for. I've been passionate about Jewish day schools, and Soviet Jewry really got to me, having both parents born in Russia and realising that their parents had the foresight to leave. I must say that my father's family left purely on the basis of not being able to practise Judaism. It wasn't an economic move.

I can't believe that I'd ever stop being involved in the Jewish community. I'd like to be a volunteer, to go to the Montefiore (old age) home. I was a volunteer guide at the Holocaust Museum until I became the president of the Executive Council of Australian Jewry. I really enjoyed that. I don't think I'll be playing bridge like my friends are, I can't imagine it.

Reminiscing about Alexandria

Joe & Racheline Barda

On the day of my visit the Bardas had begun preparing for an overseas holiday. Preparing a cappuccino in hand, Joe shows me a book on the history of the Alexandria Jewish community, with a clear sense of nostalgia and pride. He and Racheline share their memories of the golden days of the Alexandrian Jewish community and their student departure in the early fifties.

JOE: The legend is that my grandfather and his brother, at 16 or 17 years of age, walked from Libya into Egypt, having heard of the prosperity that was brought in by the Suez Canal. I suspect they were poor because my grandfather got a job as a messenger boy at a bank. Ultimately, he became the top cotton classer for that bank. He seemed to have a gift with his hands and was able to differentiate between different grades and types of cotton. He was quickly spotted by a very rich family, which was very well established in property and cotton. They formed a partnership and that company prospered. Within a few years, my grandfather, having four boys of his own, decided to form his own company and it continued to prosper. The family was extremely successful. My grandfather was a personal friend of King Fuad and when he retired from his business and King Fuad retired or abdicated in favour of his son, they used to meet in a club called the Alexandria Sporting Club. These were the years just before and during the Second World War. Things were very good in Egypt and Egyptian Jews were not troubled; they had all the freedoms. Their quality of life was fantastic.

I remember we had a lovely relationship within the community and outside the community. We were all minorities in a big Islamic world and whenever it was the Orthodox Christmas we would ring and say happy Christmas and they would ring us and say happy *Pesach*. It was a rich and tolerant society.

My grandparents were observant Jews. My grandfather knew all the prayers and used to attend *shul* regularly. He was also a member of the committee which founded the restoration of the Alexandria Synagogue. But there was pressure on families that had become established not to be too orthodox and because most of the Orthodox were the poorer Jews there was a tendency for families that had come up in society to distance themselves from that sort of image.

RACHELINE: There were some problems in Morocco for the Jews. You wouldn't call them pogroms but there were attacks on Jews. This must have been at the end of last century probably and my grandfather came to Egypt. I heard stories that they walked there. They were apparently quite well off, but when my grandfather died things got a bit difficult, but still all the kids were educated in private French Jewish schools. They moved to Alexandria where my father was working for a French firm and that's where he met my mother. Her family came from Aleppo in Syria. She was an orphan at the age of six and there were three children to look after. Her uncles helped them along until she turned 13 when, as the eldest, she went to work. Her uncle took her to somebody who falsified her birth certificate, adding two years, and she went to work as a receptionist in a place like Telecom. Then she met my father and they went on to have five children, one of whom died as an infant. Life wasn't easy. I remember growing up, we had to account for things, we were not like Joe's family, we were working class, but always with education as the aim. My parents put us through French private schools. My mother said, 'I will do anything for my children to have an education.' We had a very good life. We felt really on top and not downtrodden. We felt good, comfortable. There was a lot of respect for religion and there was such respect between communities for each other's identity that there was no conflict.

My father was an observant Jew. He prayed every day and went to shul every Friday and Saturday, and he kept kosher. We had quite a Jewish life. I remember as a kid going to synagogue every Jewish holiday. Because my grandmother was Algerian she had access to a French nationality and this was very valuable. It meant you were protected. We always had this belief that things were not going to be permanent in Egypt. My father always had the dream that he was going to migrate to France. He gave the four of us a French education to give us the baggage necessary to live in France.

Israel wasn't really considered an option. My father had a sister who married a man who migrated to Palestine from Russia. He came to Egypt on a visit, met and married her. He was an idealist. My mother had a brother who was a professional soldier, always liked to be involved in wars. After the war he became a Zionist and enrolled in the Jewish brigade and was one of the first ones to go to Israel. We didn't talk too much about this at home because it was considered dangerous. Although we had a good life we had to watch out what we were saying. I had my dreams of living in France. For me the French culture was something special.

The tensions started to develop after Israel was formed. Before then the Arabs respected the Jews. Then you would hear people in the street call you a dirty Jew and my father would say there are some problems in the city and you weren't allowed to go near that area.

JOE: I became caught more or less in the Zionist movement and became a member of a number of cells which were underground. We were concentrating at the time on sending young poor Jews to Israel and because it was illegal we had created a route via Marseille. My father would have killed me had he known I was involved. The family's prosperity depended on our contacts with the economic community. They had no intention of moving to Israel and never imagined moving from Egypt. It would have been abhorrent to my father, the thought of my being involved in a Zionist movement, absolutely abhorrent. They were not anti-Zionist, they bought land in Israel, they simply said, 'Don't get involved, it's illegal, it could cause problems to the family.' So they never knew anything about what I was doing.

In 1952 I left Egypt to go and study medicine and after one year I abandoned it and got into the family business. I then met some friends who had been to Israel and came back with a mission. They told me about it and I agreed to cooperate with them. I used to raise funds for them to enable them to carry out whatever activities they were meant to carry out. I didn't know what they were doing specifically, but in actual fact they were part of a cell which had the task to put bombs in American establishments to coincide with things like the American Day of Independence. This was meant to put tension between the Egyptian and American governments and was an official underground action of the Israeli government. It led to a huge scandal in Israel, called the Lavon Affair. These boys who were my school friends were caught and were put in jail for 20 years and I came that close also. Because my father was well-connected in the government they didn't question me. My father was able to bribe one of the officers to keep the matter quiet. It was a big crisis in my life. I was sent into exile to one of the ginning mills in the countryside. I was punished because I had this involvement and since then I felt terribly guilty that because of my position of privilege I wasn't even questioned. A lot of other people within the wider group were very severely affected, questioned, tortured, put in jail for weeks and months. The core eight or ten went through a trial, two were hanged and the others were given 20 years in jail.

RACHELINE: We found out when they were arrested. One was hanged, a couple of years before, he was an artist. I had a friend studying in an art school and he asked me if they could paint my portrait and I went there and this guy was one of the students. I picked the best portrait and it was his and I still have it today.

JOE: He hanged because he happened to be 21, so they were given the death penalty. What was significant is that these boys never said they were agents of Israel. In spite of all the torture and pressure they always maintained they were Egyptian communists. That is something which up till now when I still see them they are so proud of. They were released after 14 years and live in Israel.

In 1956 we finally decided to leave. Conditions started to be unpleasant for Jews. There were regular rock throwings and burnings and stuff liked that.

RACHELINE: People could see that it wasn't our place. But people like my parents thought there was time. I was still at school and started my final year when there was a nationalisation of the Suez Canal by Nasser and the French and English were kicked out. Joe had to leave because the old stuff would have come up to the surface. His father was worried and he had to go. October 28 was when the first bombardment started by the British and French. There was a curfew and we had to be indoors and that was for a couple of weeks. Then we were really frightened and that's when the panic started. Straight away people with French and British nationalities were told to leave within 24 hours. My grandmother was expelled, being French. My brother had just applied to a French university to study medicine and he was also expelled for that reason. It was a horrible time. My father's company was a French firm and it was closed and he was unemployed. Everyone was looking for ways to go.

JOE: My father got a phone call from the police officer who originally took the bribe saying he was being transferred and things are going to happen. He said if there's a war your son will be put in jail. Within three days I was gone to Italy and that's where I learnt of all these events in Egypt. I was isolated and alone there. I corresponded with Racheline, who was my girlfriend at the time. We met four months earlier, she was 16 and I was 20. The night before I left I told her to forget me, I didn't know what my future was going to be. The following morning from the boat I had an afterthought and I rang her and said forget everything I said to you, I want you to wait for me, I'm going to send for you.

In December my parents came to Italy. They couldn't sell anything because the family company was sequestered. They were not authorised to sell any assets above five pounds sterling so suddenly they had nothing apart from my mum's jewellery, which was sent through the diplomatic bag to Rome. That's what we lived on for two years in Italy. The company was worth 2.5 million pounds and we couldn't sell it, or the house or cars.

RACHELINE: When Joe went overseas I was very unhappy. Then his auntie came to ask for my hand in marriage so my parents thought that at least one of us will be safe. My parents were trying to sell bits of furniture and to cash in insurance to live on. We were not allowed to take any money out, only 25 pounds per person in money and 25 in gold. So I had a couple of bracelets and 24 pounds. My parents couldn't leave. They had a sister in Canada who was preparing papers for them. Things were happening all around me. My good friends disappeared from one day to the next. People left without even saying goodbye. There was an atmosphere of panic, people were meeting up and saying where are you going? Have you got a place to go? The people who didn't have a place to go went to Israel and people who had connections in Canada or America or Brazil went there. I never thought of Australia, it was really the last place.

JOE: We stayed in Italy for two years which were absolutely magnificent. But my father was in his late 40s, early 50s and he couldn't make it there. The economic conditions were bad and he didn't have any money. We tried to claim compensations but that never happened. He applied to the Egyptian government who said we were Israeli spies so they confiscated our belongings because of that. My father sold all my mother's jewellery and when that came to an end they had to do something. My parents said: 'Why don't you go to Australia as scouts and we'll follow.' So in 1958 we came to Australia and stayed with one of my uncles and got a job straight away. I was a shipping clerk and the conditions were atrocious. People were very xenophobic so there was a lot of pressure on us to adapt and conform and quickly learn the language and accents. Within six months we became fluent and things improved and my parents came. We pulled our resources together and put a deposit on a house by taking out five mortgages. My father worked as an ice-cream vendor. He had a spirit, nothing would put him down. My mother though was very severely affected. It was hard. We were all in a two-bedroom flat. We survived like that for a couple of years then we bought land and built a house and Racheline was pregnant.

I saw an ad in the paper for an assistant to the director of an export company trading with the Pacific Islands. I took the job, did well and within a short time had an offer from a big trader in New Caledonia to be a junior partner. We had two children by then and went up and stayed there for three years. There we had a beautiful life. But we didn't want our kids to be without roots. We had no roots. We had no belonging. We thought it was better we came to Australia. So I started my business in export and the kids went to a normal high school. We had the shock of our lives when Danielle went to school. The first interview we had with the headmistress she asked what scripture do you want to follow Anglican or Catholic and we said we were Jews. During scripture, they kept her for the whole time outside in the corridor where all the kids were passing. Then and there we decided we'd move to an area where we could put them in a Jewish day school and within a couple of years we moved here.

With the kids in the Jewish day school we became involved in their education and we learnt from their studies things that we had not learnt when we were young. I learnt about Jewish customs and tradition more from what my kids brought from school than what I learnt in Egypt.

RACHELINE: In Egypt some people were more observant and some people less. You didn't have the division you find here between observant and non-observant.

JOE: The atmosphere of an Ashkenazi community is different and I had to do a lot of adjusting to be able to blend in. It's different from Egypt or Turkey or North Africa. We didn't have centuries of persecution which forced the Eastern European communities closer together and closed to outside influences. I have a perception that people from Eastern Europe have a sort of siege mentality. We're open, we've never hidden our Jewishness, we almost splashed it around. We were proud of it.

We never put pressure on our kids to either conform or to accept the norm, but to question everything and to be open. And this has led all our kids to be involved in creative and sometimes not remunerative professions or activities. Whereas the siege mentality might have put pressure on kids of families of other backgrounds to be either doctors or lawyers, we didn't have that. Our one daughter is a jazz singer; my son, although he has very good skills in economics and computing, he rejects all that to be a publisher; and the youngest girl is in film. So I'm asking myself if a bit of the traditional philosophy might have led them to other professions where we would be more relaxed about the future. But on the other hand we're so proud of all their achievements.

RACHELINE: It's very important to us they marry Jewish people and we hope and pray. Although at the end of the day if they're happy we'll accept it. It was very hard when the eldest had a boyfriend who wasn't Jewish. Then there's the youngest daughter whose boyfriend is a rabbi, with strong convictions. And my son says to me, 'You're never happy!'

Helping Others

Eva Fischl

Elegantly dressed and quietly spoken, Eva sits behind the desk of her tiny office. On the wall are photos from various functions held by the organisation of which she is president, Jewish Community Services. From her early years during the Holocaust and subsequent poverty, to regained wealth, Eva's life is now dedicated to the welfare of others.

I am perplexed, interested and amazed by the fact that I'm 53, seemingly left Europe and the Holocaust that many years ago, but yet it's actually who I am. A victim of the Holocaust is still really who I am. It is the thing that actually shaped who I am, what I am, and how I behave.

I think also what defines me is that, at 53, when one sometimes looks back on things on the past, I actually never had a childhood. So that was a whole time gone. This is something you miss, you feel a lack of and, I suppose, you're an instant adult. And a lot of decisions that I have made, wrong decisions, have been made because of that.

I was actually born in 1944, within the very ghetto the Germans had set up. From there they were transporting people to Auschwitz and all the various camps. So my very birth was totally unnatural and not normal. At five weeks I was smuggled out of that place by a wonderful Czech Jewish lady for whom my family got false papers, stating that she was gentile and she was my mother. This lady lives in Israel now, on a kibbutz.

I was nearly two years old before my mother saw me again. She and my father were taken to Auschwitz, and he never came back.

My father died in Auschwitz. My mother found me again when she came back. Apparently I didn't want to call her mother, I didn't know who she was because I had obviously called this other person my mother. Obviously I don't remember that myself, it's what I am told, but knowing what we do about psychology today I can only imagine that that would have also caused all sorts of peculiar feelings of insecurity.

I ended up being the matchmaker between my mother and my future adopted father. He had lost his wife and children in the camps and was very, very depressed. I was known as the miracle child because in the whole area there were just no children left. They deemed it a good idea to send me next door, to where he lived, every day, to play, sing and dance to put a bit of life into him, and he looked forward to my visit every day. One day my mother came in and they said 'That's the mother of the girl,' and he was 17 years older then my mother, and they got married. His wish was that I did not know that he was not my father so I was brought up thinking he was. I actually found out at 14 that he wasn't. My biological father who had been killed in Auschwitz had brothers who went to Israel so at 18 I went and found them and that was an incredible quest.

Holocaust victims traditionally have a pattern, some talk about it all the time and compare everything to it. So consequently your problems are negated because you have no right to have them. So my mum was the type who referred to it often. My adopted father really wouldn't discuss it at all, to the point that one day I was in the lounge cleaning a shelf and I found photos and didn't know who they were and found out that my father had a wife and two children, because that part of their lives had never been discussed.

It's scientifically proven that children of the Holocaust suffer all this guilt and I am not in the least bit unique in this. I don't think until recently people realised how children of the Holocaust were affected. My theory is that if you had 21 years of normality, and then when there's a deviation from that normality at least your life has a pattern, you had a place in this world, your self is intact. If you're a child you really have no point of departure at all, from day one I was born into ghetto and turmoil.

After the war we escaped the communists. A lot of people forget the fact that the communists who invaded Eastern Europe changed people's lives to an untold degree. We escaped illegally when I was five, and I remember that extremely well. I remember the fear, the cold, the hunger, because we escaped by paying a guide who took you over the border and it was a very dangerous exercise — if you were discovered you were shot.

We lived for two years in Vienna and then applied for papers to America, Canada and Australia and got Australian papers. Coming here for me, in the beginning, was frankly horrendous. I hated it. I hated school. They were cruel to me at school because my sandwiches were different. My aim in life was to have a Vegemite sandwich. As a child, no one wants to be different, but European Jews were different, and remained different as we were all victims of Hitler.

You can imagine these people came here with nothing, no language and no support system to speak of. My parents were very affluent before the war. That is how they managed to save me. In fact, recently, we visited Budapest and saw the magnificent buildings my family used to own — now owned by the state.

The average Australian Jew didn't want a bar of the European migrants. We were a total embarrassment to them. We spoke differently, dressed differently. Never mind that the migrants were cultured people, educated people. My mother spoke fluent Hungarian, German and a bit of French. I felt very different because of that. Different can be unique and different can be bad, and as a child you interpret any deviance from everyone else as bad and you want to conform.

My parents didn't really know what to do and someone offered them this retail shop. It was a shoe shop and they took it for something to do and ended up with four shops. My mum really worked all her life. She's 75 and she really only stopped working three years ago. Unfortunately my father died 15 years ago.

We are doing the same thing now with the Russians. We're not really accepting them. I have an obsession with trying to do things for Russians. We, as in Jewish Community Services, meet them at the airport and give them a little gift and follow up, we run free English speaking classes. But more than that, I'm trying to really make them feel welcome and an integral part of this society. I don't know how successful we are but I'm certainly trying because that's something which I think the Australian Jews didn't do at the time for European Jews.

My communal work came about from being aware of being in a position where I don't have to work. I graduated from university and I really wanted to go on and pursue further studies at university but I've always been totally obsessed with looking after the children and being there for them. Because I was separated from my mother at birth, the psychology seems to have remained and I became obsessed with 'being there' for my children always, literally giving them what I couldn't have. But I did have the time to do something worthwhile and productive and I felt it would give me an enormous sense of satisfaction to give something back.

My parents came from observant families, probably Orthodox I'd say, and I grew up in a traditional Jewish home in terms of religion. For me, Israel is, was and remains, the miracle of our generation. That's gone on genetically because one of my daughters has gone on *aliyah*. In my household, Israel and Zionism were always an integral part of life. I have a genuine love of Judaism. With every fibre of my being, I feel incredibly Jewish.

I became involved first with United Israel Appeal because of my love of Israel. I was very involved for years in the women's division and then I worked coordinating the doctors and dentists group. I've been very involved with Wizo, was on the federal executive and now hold the position of Honorary Consultant with Wizo. I was very involved with Israel-oriented organisations. I had only recently realised that we have a lot of local needs as well, so in many ways, Jewish Community Services, the welfare organisation, was the obvious choice. The perception of the Jews is obviously of success and privilege, and that exists. Only we're not immune, be it from domestic violence, drug abuse, alcoholism, poverty, disability, mental and physical ailments. And the organisation which takes care of all those things is Jewish Community Services. I started being president of the Foundation, which was the fund-raising nest for us, and then I was elected president of the organisation. At the moment, I happen to be Federal President of Australian Jewish Community Services. I'm incidentally the first female president in 60 years plus the only Holocaust survivor.

I have my stamp which I'd like to put on the organisation. Our slogan is that we're the caring heart of the community. We are the best kept secret in the community and I would dearly like to 'expose' this secret. I'd like every Jew to know that with the utmost confidentiality and with the utmost professionalism there's a place where they can go.

If there's anything I would really like to do, if you asked me, I would really love to erase that stigma attached with having problems, that you are not a lesser person because of them. Life is not constant, it is a river that runs many courses. If I look at myself and my husband who have come from that incredible despair to a situation of privilege, the same should be regarded of people undergoing problems and crises and poverty and downfall. Hopefully, the river runs many miles and if people would look at it as not having to be a permanent situation, that it's transient and needs help. I'd like to be able to think that in some small way I was responsible for that helping push.

At the rate I'm working I might burn out. When I do I shall leave and return to my hobbies of studying languages and getting a higher degree at university. When I first graduated it was a major in psychology. But at this stage I can't do any of it because this is more than full time, it's a rare weekend when I don't have something to do with the community. At the moment I am not only NSW President of Jewish Community Services but Federal President so I am involved with that organisation around Australia and make it a point to visit the other states. As a result of my federal position I'm on the ECAJ now, I'm on the Board of Governors of the JCA and am on their Executive Appeal Committee. So really, this is like a web, it's not just Jewish Community Services. And then all organisations hold an AGM and I should represent us, and we have a lot of Jewish organisations and a lot of AGMs! So when I feel that I can't give it my all then I'll retire. I can't do anything in half measures because it's not my personality.

Journey from South Africa

Sarah Schaiowitz

Sarah greets me at the door to her sunny flat with a kind smile and prepared lunch. Intelligent and articulate, the octogenarian's home is filled with books, of which she is an avid consumer. Still bearing the thick accent of her early years in the South African countryside, she begins her story.

I was born in the Transvaal in South Africa, on a farm. My father was the country storekeeper and a manufacturer of pipe tobacco. He came from America and was introduced to my mother by her brothers. She arrived from Russia as a girl of 25 and was not yet married, so they made a match. She was a tall beautiful woman and he was a little man, he came up to her shoulders. They had six children. Two brothers had died.

My father came to South Africa in the beginning of the century, with his cousin, a man by the name of Schlesinger, the son of the original Schlesinger. They stayed in Cape Town and after a couple of years he went to a place called Natal, Durban, and opened the business. He had to go to a lawyer to draw up the contract because he was buying the business from somebody else. This contract was drawn up by a lawyer named Gandhi who had just come from Oxford to be in the Indian community and I had this important document and when I moved recently, I lost it.

My mother was Orthodox and she suffered enormously from living in the country because she kept kosher. Meat was brought in from Pretoria twice a week but it didn't satisfy her because of all the handling.

My father was very keen on education, like every other Jewish father I suppose, and the local schools were not considered good enough. I was the eldest so I was sent to boarding school at the age of 11 and the boarding school I was sent to was a convent, because, in those days, there were no other boarding schools in South Africa offering a good education. So I grew up in a convent. There were other Jewesses there whose parents were also country storekeepers. The nuns had much more tolerance for the Jewesses then they had for the Protestants, so we were not discriminated against. I learnt a little bit about Catholicism and there were those friends of mine who were fascinated by this religion. But it never appealed to me.

I had two brothers who were at a boys' high school in the same town, Pretoria, and they used to visit every Saturday afternoon, so my father took the opportunity of calling in a Hebrew teacher to come at the same time. We couldn't write because it was *Shabbat* but we had the Hebrew lessons. I suppose my mother nagged to such an extent because I don't think my father was not overly concerned. My mother was dismayed about the convent but she realised that there was nothing else.

In the country, we were perhaps the only Jewish family. There was one Jewish family, they ran the hotel. Those were the only other Jews. But when I went to boarding school, I had my aunts, my uncles, and their children living in the same town and I used to go to *shul* on *Rosh Hashana*. I used to wear my nice dress and stand outside and talk to the boys. That's what our *shul* consisted of doing in those days.

My father was very well-off at one time when he had the manufacturing business but his business went steadily down. Looking back, I think he deteriorated, he lost heart, and by the time we left, business was poor.

After I finished school, we moved to the city. We lived in a very nice house with my uncle, a brother of my mother's, a bachelor, who was very concerned with us. My sister went to university but I didn't want to go because I had a very strong responsibility to my family, to the younger ones. It wasn't something that was told to me, I just felt it. Then, later on, I did a business course, I learnt shorthand and typing.

Then my uncle opened up a millinery shop for me in the big city, in Johannesburg. In no time, I learnt how to make hats. I had this little business for some time until I got married at twenty-four.

I wanted to be married when I was young. I have a sister-in-law who was one of the early BA Honours. She was one of the early degreed women in South Africa because most women's ambition was to be married. I had ability but I was orientated toward what women were told to be.

After I got married, we remained in South Africa until 1961. My husband wanted to leave. He was a different character, a world traveller, a violinist. He'd been to India in the orchestra, he was a journalist, and he was a lawyer. He'd gone with the cricket team as a journalist to England. He was a Lithuanian boy who arrived in South Africa at the age of nine.

So we lived there and had our children there. I didn't do a thing right after I married. But when I was 42 years of age I did a four-year course through the university in Jerusalem and emerged victorious, successful, and I was teaching Hebrew.

My home was not Jewish. The kids did go to *shul* and Michael, my youngest, used to sing in the choir. My husband loved going to *shul* because he loved *chazzanus*, he was musical. Michael also went to the first Hebrew school went it opened, King David school. My brother-in-law had a lot of influence on us because my sister married this very Orthodox man, the head of Jewish education in South Africa.

The bad government came in 1948, the Nationalists, with apartheid. My husband said to me let's go to England, I don't like the look of things here. And I thought he was mad. I was not politically minded, I thought he was crazy. We had two small kids and we never had much money because he was a lawyer who was busy with everything else, he was not a money spinner. So I didn't want to go but finally he had his way and we came to Australia because Stan, our son, had come to Australia to marry a girl he'd met in South Africa. Michael, who was studying in America, wrote and said he would come to Australia but he would never come back to live in South Africa.

We moved in 1961 and it was tough for me. My husband got a job as a lawyer so he was all right but I was very miserable in the first few years until I got into the community and started teaching and got busy with social work. I got acclimatised.

In South Africa, we lived in a ghetto of Lithuanian Jews and here it was very different. I remember we had a rabbi, everyone knew of him, he was the head rabbi of South Africa, and he came here in the early 60s on a mission to collect money and he said 'Australian Jews, I didn't see one Jew there.' They were so alienated from *Yiddishkeit*.

In the beginning I was very sad, the first year I was so ambivalent. I was still finding my way and was very unsettled and after 18 months I went back on a trip to South Africa and when I came back I settled down. I wasn't keen on the South African way of living. When I think of it today I cry, when I think how little I was involved with the real situation because I think how callous can you get. My husband talked against apartheid and he wasn't unkind to blacks or whatever, but he didn't take an active role, he wanted to get away from it.

The Jews had a good life and the good life corrupts you so bad, it softens you. It somehow or other robs you of your real humanity. You live on the surface where it's all good and beautiful. We lived in false paradise. You thought you were doing your servants the biggest favour because you patronised them and they resented it and I very blushingly say to you I thought that was the way it had to be.

When we decided to leave for all the reasons that I've told you, people said to us, 'Where are you going? Who goes to Australia?' There was a joke going around then. I often repeat it, about comparing a woman in her different ages with different countries. A girl of 20 is like South Africa, innocent and ignorant; a woman of 30 is like France, very sophisticated; a woman of 40 is like Russia, mysterious; and a woman of 50 is like Australia, everybody knows where it is but nobody wants to go there. This is what people were saying to me when I was leaving.

It's an interesting story, it's the history of the Jews re-enacted in modern times. It happens over and over. Everybody has a Jewish story to tell, and in a sense it's of survival, this incredible strength to survive. I think it's the years of persecution and discrimination, it either finishes you or does the opposite.

A Public Life

Asher Joel

Asher Joel is a war veteran, journalist, former Member of Parliament and the Jew who coordinated the papal visits to Australia. Reading his resumé is a bewildering experience. So many honours and awards, page after page, that one almost becomes blasé to their significance. I am shown into his office, in the city, where the walls are covered with certificates spanning many decades of community and military service. He speaks slowly, carefully selecting his words in an unassuming manner.

My father and mother left me the greatest legacy in the world: good health, a philosophy to help others and not to aspire to ever be pretentious, to consider the small things in life to be important, and to genuinely take an interest in people's affairs.

Mine was a Jewish home but not an Orthodox one in the sense that we didn't follow kosher principles. But from the earliest age that I can recall it was always emphasised upon me that I must never ever forget that I was Jewish and should be proud of my name.

When I was a child and lived in Newtown, where I was bar mitzvahd, it was like living in a *shtetl*. Very few people had any money. It was only a handful of Jewish people who would be regarded as being affluent or having reached some position of eminence.

I didn't do very well at school. All I wanted to do was go out and work and help my mother. We were poor, and when I say poor I mean dad had to mend our shoes for us, we didn't go to the bootmaker, painted the heels with black ink. Our clothes might have been patched, but not withstanding all that, they were clothes. My parents went without to give to us. My parents only lived for us, their children. It was very difficult not having any money in the Jewish community. For instance, we didn't have a seat in the synagogue. On High Holidays my mother and father always took us to the Great Synagogue and we'd sit in the park because there was no room for us inside.

I went to work just after I turned 15 and became a messenger boy, copy boy, cadet and reporter for the *Daily Telegraph* newspaper, where I got a great deal of experience. From the most early age I realised that being in the newspaper area I would meet many people and many doors which would otherwise be closed to me would open, and in one of those doors I would find opportunities to succeed.

I had no aspirations to remain a journalist, or to be a big business-man, or to acquire great wealth. All I wanted was a comfortable existence. I never chased after, was never driven by, any ambition. I just took life as it was. I never resented poverty. It never occurred to me because I was so rich with my family life.

I can't describe nor can I emphasise too much the tremendous influence that my parents had on my life. It was a good family and we made do with things other people today would laugh at.

I always took a great interest in what was going on around me. The greatest thrill I got in my earliest days was getting my initials under a paragraph that I wrote, and that was the height of fame because bylines weren't around then. I left the *Daily Telegraph* and joined the *Labour Daily* as its parliamentary roundsman, and there of course I got thrown into the whirlpool of politics, and that's where my education really started, and particularly when I went as Lang's private secretary on two of his tours. One of the greatest men I ever knew was John T Lang; he stands out in my life as a beacon. I really knew Lang. I spent two long election trips, just Lang and me in the car, and I dealt with him in great length. We were friends until he died.

From there, I was asked by the Premier of the day, B.S.B Stevens, because I was regarded as a particularly bright and up-and-coming smart young bugger, to publicise the King George the Sixth

Coronation celebrations in 1937 which was my first entry into the affairs of public life. I always had a flair for organisation. That was the only gift I really had, the gift of spinning words and organising. It's a flair, what makes a great writer or a great artist, it's just something that's there. Protocol is simply another way of describing good manners and my mother, again back to my mother, said, 'Good manners, be respectful, call people sir' and I never minded that. And here I am, now 85 years of age, and if I admire someone I call him sir. I have no sense of subservience, it's respect. The principles that were laid down in my home influenced me tremendously.

It stood me in good stead and from then I organised the country's 150th anniversary celebrations in 1938 and just seemed to have a career in doing these things. With the exception of the King George VI Coronation celebrations and the 150th anniversary celebrations I never ever got paid for any public work that I did. These included visits by the Queen and other members of the Royal Family, the Captain Cook Bicentenary celebrations, papal visits and the opening of the Sydney Opera House. Of course, there were many spin-offs from doors which such activities opened up for me.

I could see the war was coming and decided to join the militia, so at least I would know how to defend myself. I became a sergeant and then when war broke I became the organising secretary of the Lord Mayor's War Fund and I worked very hard at that. Even though I was exempt on the grounds of occupation and age, I was now 28 years of age, I felt such a sense of duty I was determined to get back into service, into an active fighting line. So I re-enlisted in the RAF when word came through that the navy, which I had applied to join, had decided they wanted me. I finished up in MacArthur's staff right through the campaign, right through the Philippines. I met many great men and was the first Australian to be awarded the United States Bronze Star, its third highest decoration, for meritorious service in connection with combat operations.

On MacArthur's staff, I saw how public relations worked and I decided, when I came back to Australia, that I would set up public relations. So I founded PR in Australia and practised as a consultant and ran an advertising agency.

I've always been independent and would stand up to people, which always rocked them, because I believe that provided you led a decent life, an honest life, you had nothing to fear, so there was no reason you shouldn't speak up for yourself. And I've never been reluctant to take a stand. Probably a little like when the boy went to interview Disraeli, a Jewish boy, and he said 'what advice can you give?' and Disraeli said, 'There's one thing a Jew can't afford to do, that is to fail.' And what is failure? Failure is to give in, not to stand up, not to be counted.

I became very close to the Catholic Church which I found very warm and receptive. I was chairman of a committee to pay homage to Cardinal Norman Gilroy and another to farewell, on his retirement, Cardinal James Freeman. We had 500 people there and I said 'Your Eminence, as you look around here tonight you will be honoured that you have so many of your flock here, but within this flock, I assure you, there are one or two black sheep' and everybody knew what I was talking about. People admired the fact that I was always prepared to stand up and say what I was. I enjoy being a Jew. I've read a great deal on Jewish history and customs and I find it a source of pleasure, it makes me feel more responsible. I wore my badge, as a badge of honour.

I did encounter anti-Semitism but it never ever interfered with my progress. I was asked by an Irish reporter who was covering the Papal tour in 1970, 'How do you feel' — this was in front of some hundreds of press from around the world who accompanied the Pontiff — 'How do you feel as a Jew organising the Pope's visit?' And I said, 'Not a bit strange. After all, the first Pope was a Jew,' and there was a stunned silence and then a spontaneous burst of hand-clapping. As a matter of fact my papal association was probably one of the most wonderful experiences in my life, spiritually moving and an incredible opportunity to meet a human being of such international fame and respect. The Pope was a figure of such world dominance, a great man. During my lifetime the Catholics have recognised my indentification with that faith on several occasions. I received a Citation from the Archbishop of Sydney in recognition of my 'outstanding contribution to Christian ideals in public relations and the media', a unique compliment for a Jew. And then later Pope John Paul II conferred upon me Knighthood of St. Sylvester for my service to the Catholic Church. I was immensely proud of the honour and became the first Australian Jew to receive a Catholic knighthood.

I made my money as a public relations consultant, charging what I thought were reasonably high fees. I ran an advertising agency which I sold at profit; we started a business press which we sold at profit. I published a daily newspaper up at Mount Isa and started a television station and sold it successfully, certain investments which turned good. But I've never been driven by the sense of let's build buildings and make millions of dollars. The only reason I would have liked to make millions of dollars would have been to give it away.

I went to Parliament, of course, I had 21 years in Parliament. I was granted the title of Honourable, by the Queen. I was offered Cabinet positions but I didn't want to be a Cabinet minister because I'm a one man band, I don't knuckle down easy to compromise. I could never vote against my conscience, the pressures of party politics. I joined the National Country Party because they had been my chief supporters of getting a seat in the Upper House and I also enjoyed being in the association of so many men who have served in World War Two, with whom I had something in common. The President, Adrian Solomons, was a direct descendent of brothers who had been sent to Tasmania as convicts. Travelling around the country I was surprised how many Jewish descendants of early Jewish settlers and peddlers belonged to the Country Party.

I don't know what's my greatest honour, I find it hard to specify, each has its own significance. The greatest is probably the prize received for good conduct from the Newtown Synagogue when I was a kid. Of course, I was delighted when I was awarded an OBE. I also got great pleasure when told I was going to be recommended for Knighthood and become a Knight Commander of the British Empire. Before that I had the Degree of Knighthood conferred upon me and later the Order of Australia.

This sounds somewhat pompous but it isn't intended to be. I accepted these recognitions as automatic, something that happened in my life, a bit like cleaning your teeth in the morning. When Anzac

Day comes up people say 'How do you feel weighted down with so much metal?' I've got 15 medals and decorations which I'm entitled to wear according to protocol. When asked 'How did you come to get them?' my reply is that 'After you get the first, the rest come easy.'

I've been president, vice-president and honorary fellow of many bodies. These have included the first honorary fellow of the International College of Dentists and the degree of Honorary Doctor of Letters from Macquarie University.

During the course of my life I have met many prominent and interesting people: the Queen and other members of the Royal Family, American Presidents Johnson, Nixon and Bush. They're all big people. But they're just people, they're normal. It's a concept in the eyes of the public that these personalities are above everybody. Big people don't have to be above everybody, big people are big, full stop. They don't have to worry about competition. They're gracious, nice, decent. They're ordinary. They eat, they drink, they sleep, they defecate.

I haven't mentioned my wife to whom also I owe much. I owe as much to my wife as to my parents, but in some respects more so because through thick and thin for nearly 50 years she's stood by, she's encouraged me, she's never given me any reason at any time to doubt her integrity, her sense of values, and her completely unaffected attitude to life. On her side, our children are sixth generation Australians. There's not many Jewish families like that. She has ancestors going right back to a convict boy who arrived at the age of 14 and became the first Jewish alderman of Hobart.

The Jewish community will survive but it will increasingly compromise to the demands of modern life and *Yiddishkeit* will be hard to maintain. Jewish children growing up in the atmosphere of Australia, like the children of other cultural groups, will meld into the Australian way of life. The younger generation who don't understand Hebrew don't want to come to synagogue and follow, parrot fashion, the service, hence the growing popularity of reform. The question of intermarriage will have to be faced. There will have to be, I believe, a relaxation in the acceptance of children of parents where one is not Jewish, otherwise we will disappear. The United States has shown that the number of Orthodox is diminishing compared with the number of Temple-goers. Me, I'm still old fashioned, I like going to the Great, I like *davening*. But then, that's nostalgia.

There is so much more I would have liked to have done, so many areas and activities, avenues, where one can do something. I have not enough years to fulfil what I would like to achieve. For instance, I met Princess Diana several times. Here was someone who was not intellectually great, who was regarded by some people as a lightweight, who was born with a charisma that reached up and touched people and helped people. It's a magical quality and I envy the way she was able to do it. There are people who do this and are gifted like this and aren't important or well known; their mere presence gives people confidence; makes their life worth living.

I've thought about life a great deal and I think it's all summed up in Maimonides' Thirteen Principles of Faith when we say 'I believe in the creator, blessed be his name. He is, was and always will be.' And it's this glorious acknowledgment of something that is beyond that makes it so easy to be a Jew. And I have never considered asking God for anything. I don't believe in praying for something. The Almighty has too many other things to worry about it.

DIASPORA WITH A CENTRE: THE POST-WAR GENERATION

Rethinking Priorities

Henry Kinstlinger

Henry is a doer, a problem-solver. His arrival at the Yeshiva several years ago, as its public face, has transformed the organisation's image, through his coordination of many and varied successful public events and celebrations. He is a jovial man who seems unlikely to have six children and a strictly Orthodox home. We sit in the dining room where he begins his story and then, surrounded by active kids, we retreat to the family room to complete the interview.

It's a classic migrant story. My parents and myself were born in Poland and came to Australia when I was two years old. We started off in Redfern. My parents bought whatever fruit was left over at the end of the week before it got tossed out and we lived on that. My parents have since passed on. My father died when I was 20 and my mother eight months later.

They both went through the Holocaust, were previously married and brought up their own families. Interestingly, they were childhood sweethearts before they married and had separate families and they got together again after the war.

We never spoke of the Holocaust or that period of their lives at home. It was never brought up by myself or my sister. We were aware of what they went through. It wasn't until they both passed away, and we were going through old documents, that we actually saw the names of their children, and when they were born, their old birth certificates and marriage certificates. So the history is there but we've never dwelled on the past, we've always looked at what we have today and how we can apply the past and what we're going to have tomorrow.

My family was small 'r' religious. My father was a member of the *Yeshiva*. He was a Monumental Mason. We made *kiddush* Friday night and we had *Seder* and we walked to *shul* on *Yom Kippur* and *Rosh Hashana*, but it wasn't an overly religious household. Saturday afternoons were spent watching the wrestling.

I was an individualist. I would never conform to society's rules. I had my own way of doing things and it took time for me to actually find myself. I rode a motorcycle. I almost killed myself on it. I bred a German guard dog. I was a bit of a stirrer, I was good for a laugh, and I haven't lost that. I've had ribs broken at anti-apartheid demos; I was extensively involved in the moratorium movement; I was the coordinator of a group in Sydney High called SHAG, Sydney High Action Group. I thought it was a good idea to organise strikes and walkouts from school, which is one of the reasons I wasn't welcome to return to that school in Year Five.

I had no intention of being anything at school. Career wasn't important to me. I was living for the moment. I was heavily involved in the Zionist movement, in *Betar*. I had my own office where I was developing camp notes and programs. That was at school. If there was any learning involved it was coincidental. In that year, my intention would have been to go to Israel, come back for a few years, and then eventually make *aliyah*. But I had no idea what career path I wanted to take. I certainly didn't want a university path.

In 1973, I had the opportunity to go to Israel, an opportunity which should not be missed. It was Israel's 25th anniversary. So instead of finishing my higher school certificate I went to Israel with all the best intentions of coming back and doing it at tech. I had a great year, they threw in a war for good measure, which was an amazing experience in its own right.

My year in Israel was very full-on from a Zionist perspective, the marches, parades, conferences, and the war. We were in the Sinai and we were *davening* on *Kol Nidrei*, planes were flying 200 to 300 feet overhead, south. We had no idea what was going on. We woke up in the morning and there was no one left there, they all got called up to their units. We had a skeleton staff, they issued us arms, taught us to shoot in the sand dunes, and next thing we were doing *shmira* and going to concerts in the local air base. I remember writing letters: 'To whom it may concern, if I don't return' ... Thank God the letters were not delivered.

I didn't go back to school when I came back. Instead, I started selling encyclopedias door to door. I was very successful but decided to join my sister and brother-in-law in a printing business. We had a $1.5 million turnover and staff of 15 to 20.

I stayed with them until we lost my son in 1980, where we had a turn around in our lives. We went from being traditional Jews to Orthodox Jews. We went from Australia to Zfat in Israel, where we spent about six months. From there we went to *Yerushalayim*, had a few children in *Yerushalayim*. Spent a total of five years in Israel.

He was our first child. It was a month after his second birthday. We had three gates from the house leading to the swimming pool where we were renting. Somehow all three gates got left open. He made his way out there, was playing with the ball and we assume the ball fell in the pool and he went to get it. I was at work, it was Friday morning at 9 am. It's interesting when you look back after 12 years now you see how your life has turned around, changed, and you can apply all of that directly to that one tragedy.

I went to a conference recently and one of the throw-away lines was, 'The greatest gift is wrapped in the greatest problem.' It could have ruined us, as tragedies like this unfortunately ruin many families. But we accepted there was some greater purpose to what had happened and to try to put that purpose into reality required us to become religious, to go to Israel, spend time there to find ourselves. And we did. We found ourselves and our *Yiddishkeit*. Ruth went to a ladies' seminary and I went to *kolel*.

I left the printing business on the basis that I would have an ongoing pension, funds would keep coming to support us. But those funds didn't come. Nothing came at all. My brother-in-law divorced my sister, he had my power of attorney and he sold the business, and I ended up being totally broke. That wasn't a state of mind conducive to learning, so I had to survive.

I played the money market. I found loopholes in the Conversion Act. I survived playing the black market, if you like. I survived by my wits. I set up on my own. I could mix it with the best of them in business in Israel. You do what you need to do to survive. And I'm not suggesting what I was doing was necessarily illegal, but the morals there are just so much laxer than they are here.

Life didn't settle down for us, always a struggle. You work a six-day week and if you're Orthodox the only day left is *Shabbat*. So there was virtually no free time. It was either work or *Shabbat* or work or *Shabbat* and you're always under pressure. Unless you go to Israel with a pioneering attitude and expect the hardships that a pioneer would expect you are disillusioned. In the end, when I went there I had a businessman's mind-set, not a pioneering mind-set.

They were difficult years. We had to deal with the loss of a child, I had to establish myself in business, and became an insulin dependent diabetic, which got misdiagnosed — I was sent out of hospital after two weeks with the wrong treatment. So when the opportunity with Yeshiva came it was time to come back.

I felt like I owed something to the Yeshiva for the connections they made for me in Israel before we left. So I spent the last two weeks before I went to Israel writing a fund-raising management program for them and that impressed them. They knew that I was capable and they needed someone who could do what I do. It was once again an opportunity which shouldn't be missed. So I came back and have been working for the Yeshiva now for seven years.

Yoram Sforay, he's the Israeli journalist that infiltrated the neo-Nazi movement — I was his minder — came up with my job description very well. He said 'Henry, you're the consulier. The consulier is the guy who gets the job done.' I have no job description, basically just do the job. Whatever needs to be done, get it done. I'm the fireman, I'm the public relations officer, and the Yeshiva spokesperson.

I've been fortunate enough to be able to apply the various skills which I've developed over the years — photography, videography, computers, marketing, printing, advertising and public relations, which all are linked into my role at Yeshiva where I now work as Special Projects Director, and most recently was nominated to the board.

When I first joined, people looked at the Yeshiva very stereotypically and they didn't understand it. And the Yeshiva really could live up to that stereotype. But over the years the whole perception of the Yeshiva from the community's eyes has changed and I'd like to think I've had a lot to do with that.

Someone once said — and it's not the Yeshiva's quote — that the Yeshiva is the Jewish soul of Sydney. Take the Yeshiva away, take what the Yeshiva has done over the last 15 to 20 years and what have you got left?

There are no levels in Orthodoxy: you either observe the *mitzvot* or you don't. You're not there to pick and choose. I maintain the spirit of the law in everything I do, not only in the active commandments but in the way I interact with my fellow human beings. But it's not a label. You're not Conservative, you're not Reform, you're not Orthodox, you either accept it, and if you do accept it, how do you apply it to your day-to-day living?

The more you water down your *Yiddishkeit* the less chance you have of having a Jewish great-grandchild. You look at Reform. How many Reform great-great-grandparents are there?

Today there is in fact a strong resurgency of Orthodoxy. The children are going back, looking for that Jewish spark. They're looking for spirituality in modern society and the way they live. That's why the greatest number of people in the Krishna movement and alike are Jewish. They just found the wrong spiritual link. People are looking to come back, they're realising what their parents had and they don't want to lose that.

Orthodoxy is very good for family life. Your children are protected, they're not exposed to the influences that are out there. You ask my children what rave is, they don't know what rave is. It's a nice safe environment. I see kids who grow up in this sort of environment. They get married and have kids and they're happy. They may not be happy doing the things that you'd like to do, so what? Don't thrust your values on me and I won't thrust mine on yours. But be happy with what you've chosen and if you're not happy with what you've chosen, keep looking, because what's right for you is usually just around the corner. You just have to be able to see it when it's there.

I firmly believe that everything we do is a piece of the puzzle. You look at my family today, that's come out of tragedy. That's the foundation of my faith. It's my basic outlook on life. I'm a fairly happy person. I see the positive in all situations no matter how hard that situation might be. You have to look beyond what's staring you in the face, look around it, over it, and through it. And I do my best, always. If you do your best you can have no regrets because you could not have done better. And that's with everything, with family, with work, with your friends.

I want to see my family grow and develop and extend that which they have learnt from me. I look at my children and I see my personality in each one. I see my humour, the way they deal with situations, their confidence, and that's my legacy, that's certainly my legacy.

Do I genuinely believe the *Mashiach* will come? I certainly believe the *Mashiach* has not come and I believe the *Mashiach* will come. However, I'm not in a position to be able to predict when. You can't pick and choose. The belief in *Mashiach* is a fundamental belief that we have as Jews. If you consider yourself a Jew and believe that Judaism is linked to God, then you can't reject it. How you apply it is up to you but as far as belief and acceptance are concerned, there is no question.

A Woman's World

Miriam Frommer

Miriam is the daughter of a modern Orthodox rabbi, and is finding expression as a feminist within Conservative Judaism. In the lounge room of their spacious suburban house, Miriam's husband packs away his medical papers and offers me a cold drink before leaving us undisturbed.

It was only as an adult that I was really able to follow my own path. I could not do it as a child living under my father's roof, which I guess is not surprising in anybody who has a father who is a public figure. My father was an Orthodox rabbi and he was in a number of small communities in Australia from when I was a child. But the one that I remember most vividly is growing up in Brisbane.

He was the only Orthodox rabbi there and I have memories in my childhood for example of sitting next to the Premier of Queensland on the viewing platform on Anzac day.

He had been educated as a lawyer in Germany and he got to the stage virtually where he could have been a judge but because of the Nazis he was unable to practise in that profession and he then acquired a second qualification, as a rabbi. But his father had been a rabbi and he was always very interested in Judaism, unlike my mother who came from a totally assimilated background.

He had a very broad secular education in the classics so his whole outlook was sort of Western, secular democratic. He was personally a very tolerant and diplomatic person, a very affectionate person. I guess having daughters and not sons, and especially my being the oldest and intellectually inclined and very interested in religion, he taught me all the things that I suppose he would have taught a son.

As a child I accepted the whole kaboodle, I had no problems with it at all. In fact I loved it. I loved it to such an extent that when my father used to do the bar mitzvah lessons in our home when I was a small child I used to beg my parents to let me sit on the doorstep outside, which I did. I still remember sitting in my nightie outside, hearing all this so by the time I got to do my own bat mitzvah I knew the whole thing because I'd been through it three or four times in the previous years.

But I think I was under a lot of pressure being Rabbi Fabian's daughter. *Kashrut* was something that was imposed on me, living in a rabbi's home. When I was at university I had already decided that I would not continue as stringently and I started eating out. And that was difficult while I was still living at home but once I went to London I could eat whatever I liked wherever I liked. I started eating out a little bit more in non-kosher restaurants. One of the things I remember vividly is, when I was living in London, the unbelievable freedom that nobody knew what I was doing on Saturdays. I mean I could just hop on the train and it really didn't matter. Things I could never have done in Australia. I just didn't feel those particular things I was giving up were very important I suppose.

I really didn't question any of the theology until much much later in life, until my father became ill prior to his death in 1989. One of the things that I found was when I was going through a phase of not knowing whether I believed a lot of things, I had to keep coming back and telling myself that my father believed these things and I respected his intellect so there must be something in it. I have been on that type of treadmill for a lot of the time.

It's only in my adult years that I've been able to thrash this out, mainly with my mother, and we've talked about a lot of these things and she's tried to explain to me that, especially as she came from an unorthodox background she was very unsure of herself, and being a totally non-aggressive person anyway she just didn't have it in her to challenge people and confront these issues. I think they were just too difficult.

The thing that I always say is those aspects of the traditional beliefs which just relate to things that happened in the past, it really doesn't make any difference to my everyday life whether I believe them or not. I mean whether or not Noah's ark did float for 40 days is completely irrelevant to anybody's life so who cares. It may be true, it may not be true, it doesn't make any difference, but there are other things in the Torah which make an enormous difference.

One of these is the attitude to women and there's no way the type of God that I was brought up to believe in can be reconciled with the attitudes of people. There's no way that I can accept any of this. I'm perfectly prepared to say that the source of those ideas was divine and that somehow God, whatever God means, communicated those particular ideas. Even if Moses was a pure transmitter and didn't tamper with it, the people to whom he communicated and the people who eventually wrote it down injected their own values into it, somehow or other. This is what the progressives would say — there's a lot of good stuff there but you have to recognise that it has been influenced by humans, it is a human document. The whole thing is a people-product and people are men unfortunately.

One of the puzzles that I never sorted out in my own head but I think it's very true for women in my generation, is why we didn't question our lack of equality in Jewish practice, even in our early twenties. The irony is that this has all happened while the feminist movement had liberated women in their secular lives and I'm one of those women who has experienced the benefits, who has been convinced of the need for change and who has participated in this movement and who has pushed for change in my personal life and in my professional life.

My father was an absolute feminist. There was no question about it. His office was at home and so he was a great help around the house by virtue of the fact that my mother and he were very much a partnership. He didn't see people as having predetermined roles in life and he was an involved father. The interesting thing about him is that he lost both his parents when he was 10 and family was very important to him, something he really cherished.

I'm a biologist and this whole concept that women who are menstruating are somehow unclean in the ritual sense and have to do something to rectify that situation is something which I reject totally. I totally reject practices which discriminate against women on the basis of their biology and I view them as being the product of primitive times.

What I find the least reasonable is that this God who is supposedly behind all this didn't realise what the impact was going to be on men. Men don't need an excuse to discriminate against women, and here you're giving them a beautiful one and we can see it in our texts. I don't blame the people 3,000 years ago, they couldn't have known any better, but what I absolutely fail to be able to accept is that you can base present practice on past precedents which have been shown to be flawed or no longer relevant.

I have sort of made it my professional occupation to publicly challenge a lot of the assumptions about Orthodoxy. And even though I appear to people to be extremely self-confident and assertive in fact I'm extremely diffident and I usually end up in tears after I've sounded off at one of these public occasions about these issues, especially if I've had a hostile response. I'm getting better but I've had lots and lots of hostile responses. It's happened to me recently and I'm better now at handling that situation and saying to them I just disagree with your point of view and I don't think you have it right for women. They can't imagine that people actually find a lot of this stuff unpleasant and alienating. There's a great unwillingness on the part of the rabbis to meet people where they are at, to talk with people about their concerns about the religion and it's very much a case of you just be good and you just make sure you buy the right brand of salami and everything will be OK and it just totally glosses over so many other questions that people have. I'm very much inclined towards the Judaism which talks about social justice and the ethical dimensions. That's the thing my father was all about. One of his favourite lines was about 'doing justly, and loving mercy'.

Being my father's daughter, I am very idealistic about the mission of the Jews as being a light unto the nations and that has absolutely nothing to do with whether you eat kosher salami, it has to do with modelling particular kinds of ethical behaviour and maybe keeping kosher is a part of that ethical behaviour.

But my husband and my children keep saying to me, stop banging your head against a brick wall, just accept the fact that you are not Orthodox, the views that you are espousing are not Orthodox views, you are not going to convert the Orthodox to your point of view so if you can't beat the Orthodox, join the Liberal — and I eventually did that.

The fact that women were treated in what I consider to be a very unjust way in Orthodox Judaism was something I could have got around by just joining the Liberal synagogue but it took me years to get to the point where I was able to do that. Not because I care about what people think, because it doesn't worry me in the least, but I felt that I ought to try and struggle more from within.

I have found my home, it's egalitarian, it's inclusive, it's not about telling people they shall or shall not do. It's about telling people about Judaism in a mutually cooperative way and it's completely different from what I would get from the large Orthodox synagogue for example. It's a thriving place. I found a middle ground that's comfortable in terms of practice.

We have lots of discussions about Jewish continuity and how much do you need to do to pass on a sufficient quantum of Judaism to the next generation and it's undoubtedly true that people who grow up in an observant household, as my husband and I did, are more likely to produce observant children than our children, who grew up in a less observant household. There's a dilution down the line but that's true of the whole world except for the people now returning. As Dennis Prager has said beautifully, the non-Jews are too nice, we have so much in common with our non-Jewish co-workers and co-students that unless there's a very strong reason to remain Jewish — and I'm not sure how you give people that reason.

The result of growing up in our particular home is that our children are all sceptics because they've got two parents who are scientists but neither I nor my husband have ever put Judaism down. We both value it. It's in our blood. We have a strong emotional tie and there's things we believe very strongly. When the children were growing up I consciously took them to *shul*. So they're very aware of their heritage. But I'm allowing them to make a choice because I don't think you can force religion on people. I wouldn't ever do it. If my children make choices, I accept responsibility that I brought them up to think for themselves and I have to hope. I would far prefer they marry Jews for a whole lot of reasons, some practical, some emotional, but I do recognise that in a free society people have freedom.

I've had quite direct discussions with them and I've said do you think you'd marry Jews and all three have said yes and they've given me various reasons and I have to leave it to them. If they married out I'd feel disappointed and be wary, depending on who the person was; how much cultural similarity there was, but I can't argue with someone who tells me they've found a non-Jewish person who's a good person rather then be pushed into a marriage with someone simply because they're Jewish. I guess only time will tell how the positives and negatives weigh up. But we haven't said to them don't you dare marry out or I'll disown you. When I was a student I flatted with a lady who had severed relations with a child who married out and I begged her to take that child back and she wouldn't. It's like closing the stable door after the horse has bolted. We'll see how our children slot into whatever community there is ten years down the line. We live in interesting times.

Making Do

Zina Satanovskaia

As with many emigrants from the former Soviet Union, Zina lives a frugal lifestyle, in a housing commission town house. I was introduced to her by Mimi, a social worker with Jewish Community Services which provides assistance to Zina in caring for her son, Sasha, who is 16 and severely intellectually disabled. Despite her constant worries, she appears cheerful and speaks English far better then she believes she does. We are joined at the dining table by Gennadi, her 15-year-old son, and sporadically by Sasha, who runs in and out of the room, often with Gennadi following, keeping a watchful eye.

My family are from Russia, it's a part of Russia, Ukraine. My father lived in a small Jewish city, like a village, like a *shtetl*. My grandparents were cousins.

Before the revolution, my father's father was injured and he couldn't work after this. My father and his brother started working from a small age but my father wanted his smallest brother to learn and he sent him to Yiddish school in the synagogue. And my father did his homework and he started to learn with him and that was his school. Then there was revolution in Russia and everything was changed.

My mother was born in another little *shtetl* and her father was a communist and he worked in big works. But when the war started, the first day, my grandfather went to the war and they didn't know about him anymore. Her mother, she was dead, there was a bombing in the village. From the first day of war, she was left with her sister.

She was 16 and her sister was nine. From the first day her *shtetl* it became a ghetto by the Nazis.

My father had to go to the army and he was taken prisoner and then he escaped and he went to find what happened to his parents. But they were dead and he was taken to this ghetto too, where he met my mother.

It was romantic for them because they had a wedding, a *chuppa,* even in the ghetto. They were in the ghetto for four years. Every day, they lived just for that day. Our father, he told us a lot about it because it was very difficult time for them. They lost all their family. I don't know what it is to have grandparents. I miss that. My father had to bring up my auntie, she was just nine years old, and after the ghetto, he wanted her to have some education.

It was difficult after the war, they didn't know where they could live and the money and place where they could live and to find a job and find a life. They stayed in the same place after the war because my mum was born there and they moved only when I was six years old because my father had relatives in Odessa. My father had a heart attack, he couldn't work any more. So we had to move to a city where someone could help us, and start a new life. But my father after this, for a long time, he was a sick man. He worked but it was difficult, but he had to do this for family, for children. He was a hairdresser. My mother had to do every job she could find, in fabrics, small businesses. We weren't poor but in Russia it was not easy.

My father liked so much everything Jewish. He could read Hebrew and me and my sister we could write Hebrew and read Hebrew books and all time they spoke Yiddish, my mother and father. They were religious before but after it was very difficult in Russia with religion. But we celebrated big *Yom Tovs,* we went to synagogue. But it was impossible to be religious.

I didn't feel different at school, I was friendly with everyone. But after school when I wanted to go to university, I had my exams and the teacher who took this exam, he was a Jew too, he said, 'You can't go to the university.' He told me that we had enough Jewish people in university and it was terrible, I was crying. It was a shock for me but he didn't want to listen, to know. I wanted to be a fashion designer.

Instead I took this result of my exam and went to college for building, a special course, because I had a good result and after this I could work like an engineer. It was a long course, for four years, and I studied architecture and for building and for commercial buildings. And I worked like in an institute; they did everything, preparation for starting buildings. I enjoyed working because I liked graphic design and drafting. It was an interesting job.

After I married, I wished to have babies but my two babies they were born dead, my first two children. Life was very difficult. You have to live in small houses with parents, all together. We live with our parents in a one-bedroom flat and there wasn't a toilet in the house, you had to go down the street. There were 12 flats and one toilet in the street and in winter it was cold and no water, it was frozen.

We weren't a religious family but we kept some traditions. In Russia, you couldn't be really religious. There wasn't kosher food to buy. We couldn't openly go to the synagogue. My father had his own place in synagogue but only went for the big *Yom Tov*. It wasn't very openly celebrated. It was not possible to be religious but I think it's not so important. It's what you feel in your heart is more important.

We started thinking about leaving when my nephew started growing up and we started thinking about his future and about our future. At this time, I started thinking, my first child died and we were thinking maybe we could change our life for the better, before we were old, while we could do something about it. And we started talking to our father about it. But he was scared to go somewhere. My father started his life many times, again and again. You don't understand what it means. It was very different in Russia than here. People were happy with a small good piece in life. Because when you have something you think maybe it will disappear. When you emigrate you have to leave everything, take nothing, just a few pieces of clothes. You can't take money because it can't be exchanged, you have to leave it.

So we stopped thinking about this, and started living in Russia again. Then my second child died and then my Sasha was born. He's unfortunately a sick boy, he is now sixteen. It's still today we don't know what's wrong. We did everything you can do in Russia. We went to different places, to Moscow. It was the biggest place where you can find more institutions, they can find maybe something. They did a lot of tests here which show nothing. In Russia they don't know exactly with him but they did for him some injections, massages, and he was all times for some medical treatments. He's now more better. Now he has no treatment. In Russia they didn't think about him. They said, 'You do this' and you do it. He was scared. I can't go to doctor with him now, he's still scared of them.

He's more intellectually disabled because he can't talk. He can just speak a few words. I understand him but it's difficult for other people. It's four years now that he goes to school. Now he understands English at school, but it's very difficult to understand sometimes what he wants; difficult to explain. That's why he becomes nervous now, with age he becomes aggressive. At the same time, he's a very good boy because we're not a long time here and it's difficult for me to find the right way for him, the future with him. But there are more ways here than Russia.

When my father died, it was hard for us. We lost our father. It was a deep pain for me, my sister, my mum. She was very dependent on him in all the time they were together and always my father decided what to do. He was first in the family and it was difficult on my mother.

After this was the war between Russia and Afghanistan and in Russia it was all boys had to go to the army for three or four years. My nephew was 17 when we started thinking of leaving. He was like my child too. We are very close.

My brother-in-law, he had his cousin in Australia. And they decided to go to his cousin and they went to Austria then applied to Australia. To Australia just a few families can immigrate. But it was their luck that his cousin paid money for them to be here. And when they came to Australia, they understand that we can't emigrate there. It was impossible, the answer was 'no'. The big problem was Sasha. First, you had to apply on some paper: who you are, what you do, everything, and it wasn't enough for us.

Then there was Jewish welfare, they did a big job for people from Russia, for the family to be together. It was Special Assistance Category program and we were first because my sister went every day to welfare and talked to everyone and tried to do everything for us. Jewish welfare did a great job.

I was in shock when I found out I was coming to Australia. I could not believe in this. It was a very great day. For me it's great we can change our lives for the better.

When we came to Australia I chose the nearest school for Gennadi, near my flat. It was a short walk to the school and I could go with him, drop him off and pick him up. Sasha also started school. After he had a lot of tests, the government found a school, now he goes to special school every day. It's great, it's everything for me, here is everything for me.

But then we had big problem with a very unkind neighbour. Terrible. We couldn't live there, we have to move, but we couldn't find how. We had to leave for safety for our lives. She threatened us. It is difficult with Sasha with renting. Not everyone likes it. He started knocking on doors. He screams loudly when he is nervous. But we were lucky for three years, it was a good place where we lived, good people all around. But then the place was sold and the people who bought it wanted to live there. They gave us just two weeks to move. It was impossible. At this time I was on the waiting list in the Department of Housing and they put Sasha on immediate housing. I started to go every day to the Department of Housing because I could find nothing and after that they found this place for us. It's luxury. I would be more happier to buy our own place one day. Maybe it can happen. A small place, but your own.

My youngest son, Gennadi, is my light, after everything I've been through. My husband and I are now separated because it's difficult. We changed everything. Maybe it's easier for me because I study English at school and it helped me but it is difficult for him with English, difficult to find a job, to understand. But maybe we need some time. But we're still good parents for our children. He comes every day to help with Sasha and Gennadi because I have no time to learn, study. Now he tries to find some jobs with Russian people. He's a good painter but he can't speak English and he can't drive and jobs depend on a car. Because he's a very good painter, if he can understand and study English and drive a car he can find a job after that.

I'm very optimistic about the future because I wait every day that sometimes it will be better and better for me because the first miracle is that we are here. I am with my sister and my mum and now with my auntie here soon too. For my mum it's a bit easier and I hope maybe, sometime soon, something good for Sasha for the better. It's a big pain for me worrying about the future but I hope my Gennadi if he understands me and does everything right he will have a good future.

I remember my father, and I did what he would have liked, for my son Gennadi to go to the Jewish school. When he was a small boy my father died but he taught him Yiddish and explained to him all the tradition and it was very interesting for him.

He went to the Jewish Board of Education summer camp and the principal of this camp got me to go to a Jewish school. I went to talk to the principal, a very nice person. I talked to him about my life and he wanted to talk to Gennadi and he talked to him and took him into the school. So nice, like a family, one class, a very nice place. I was so happy.

Then Gennadi started preparing for his bar mitzvah and he started lessons. Gennadi hasn't had a *bris* and he can't have it because he was very sick boy in Russia; he got a lot of allergies, and we couldn't do anything. My father wanted him to do a *bris* but it was impossible for him. Now it's difficult to change this and I am doing everything to prepare him for his bar mitzvah. I told the Rabbi the truth, I told him what Gennadi means to me, and he started teaching him. He went every Sunday to lessons, he learnt everything for the bar mitzvah, he prepared. We have a date for his bar mitzvah, everything was ready, and when it was close to his bar mitzvah they said if he didn't do a *bris* he couldn't do it. So we did him a bar mitzvah with our family at home. For me it was a shock. I said to the rabbi 'maybe you can do something for him. I didn't lie to you. I waited and waited so much and Gennadi waited for this so much.' Anyway it was nice. Gennadi invited all his friends we did everything at home.

Now it's impossible for me to visit Russia. I wanted so much to one day go and visit the grave of my father. Maybe one day, but now I depend very much on Sasha: I can't leave him, can't go somewhere at night, have to be with him all time. It's good he goes to school. But school will stop when he will be 17 and then what will happen I don't know. We're not here a long time and he's on waiting lists everywhere.

I have no time to go looking for a job. I'm very busy with my family, looking after them, because now my mum has her own place, Department of Housing, with my auntie, but she has to be sometimes with me and I have to look after her. She is very sick.

One year ago I went to Jewish Community Services and asked them about help. Mimi, she is a great person who works there, she found for Sasha (and Jewish Welfare paid for this) like a baby sitter. A very nice young man, he came every Friday to my place from 7 to 10 and he took Sasha, and Gennadi went as well, and they went to visit places: the bowling club, sometimes to the cinema, and Sasha likes him so much, he's a very good person. It gives me two hours for myself and it is important to Sasha, who needs a long time to talk to a new person; it's difficult for him with a stranger.

I'm a little sad for Gennadi because he feels the difference at school. Many people from South Africa there think it's our fault that we are poor in Australia. But we are not poor, we can have everything necessary for our lives because we know what it is not to have these things. But we live this life and we understand you can live without it and be happy.

People came here from Russia, they are all engineers, doctors, they all have a good education, and they started working and do everything here, washing places, washing dishes, everything, and they don't care about this. A lot of people who live here immigrated 20 years ago. The first people from Russia live in their own places, they pay mortgage, maybe it would be great for us one day.

It's bad that people think about us as different. It's our life. What our parents lost in their lives it's terrible. They lost everything and all the time they started their life again. We started our life from zero here too, we had everything necessary for our lives in Russia.

Happy-Go-Lucky

Tom Budai

I met Tom several years ago at a meeting where he represented Shamash, a social group set up by Jewish Community Services to cater for Jewish people with intellectual disabilities. To describe him as friendly would be understating Tom's permanently cheerful and friendly demeanour. He is forthright, and polite. On this evening, I sit with Tom, who is several months from celebrating his 40th birthday, and his mother, at the dining table of their home, and Tom tells me about aspects of his life.

I work all week in a law firm as a courier. I have a girlfriend, Roxanne, I have known her two years now. Roxanne is living now in Malabar. I met her in group. She's very nice.

I went to school in Belmont. After, I went to Tempe, then Arncliffe, then Warrowa. About age 13 I finished school, went to work with mother in a menswear shop, then a law firm after that. I have been there 14 years as courier. I go all round the city. I know my way very well; know the lawyers and barristers, enjoy it very much, I talk to people at work. I come home in the afternoon when I finish. I leave home about 5.30 in the morning, go in, open up. I finish at 5.00 in the afternoon.

I have two brothers, one in Terry Hill, the other one in Castle Craig. One is 50, I don't know how old the other one is, my mother would know. I've got a sister-in-law. From my first brother I have one sister-in-law. I've got three sisters-in-law from my other brother, he's been married three times. I've got two nephews and two nieces. One is about 31, I think, the other one is 18. One nephew is married. I went to the wedding in Denmark. I've been flying many times, to Israel, Hawaii, Christchurch, Auckland, Melbourne, been around the city. Israel — I went there in 1975, very nice. We went on a bus tour, it was very hard to walk there because couldn't go too far in borders. We went to a kibbutz there, very nice place.

I met my girlfriend in a social group. It was run by Jewish Community Services, used to be run by them, but not any more. Now it's run by the *Shamash* group. I was leader of the group but I don't go any more, it's too much trouble, too much hard work, very hard to look after that group.

Jewish Community Services helps people bring out the new people from Russia who come here. They have a workshop for printing now, and help people to get into a home. They helped *Shamash*. I was group leader, I looked after the group, got meetings organised. I used to go to Circular Quay on the ferry, things like that. I first started as a member. It was a good time. I read about them in the Jewish paper and called up. We used to go on outings, about ten of us.

One day, a lady who worked there asked me to look after the group. So I did. I used to go to all the meetings of Jewish Young Adult Forum, we met to talk about how to organise things.

I like being Jewish. I go to synagogue. There are three different kinds of Jews: the kosher ones, non-kosher ones, and the really kosher ones — the ones with the big hats. They can't watch TV on Saturday. I'm a normal one, liberal, that's better. It's hard to eat kosher food all the time, very hard. My cousin used to but he gave up, it was too much hard work to look after a kosher kitchen. I got normal, that's a better way to be.

We have *Channukah*, Passover, *Purim*. I go to synagogue in September. I don't go to synagogue every week, only on High Holidays. I enjoy it very much, I read the book, hear the rabbi talking. You meet lots of people in synagogue. I go to *Moriah* at the moment because the other synagogue was burnt down. Rabbi Franklin and the other, Rabbi Ingram, are there. I went to the Rabbi's house for a party, something to do with *Succah*. He is a very nice guy too, singing, eating. I had a bar mitzvah at home but don't remember much, people brought presents.

During *Channukah*, we light the candles every night a different candle. At *purim* you dress up, beautiful. Yeah, I like *purim*. Passover you eat plenty of *matzah*. I learnt that at school. A Jewish teacher came once a week, Abigail was her name. It used to be good, scripture classes.

I watch TV every night. I watch the news, what happens in Israel. It's not going well there at the moment.

I'm forty. It's good to be happy. Just keep smiling and be happy.

Finding Her Place

Ella Dreyfus

With her husband and two children, Ella lives apart from the main Jewish population, in a suburb where there are too few Jewish people to warrant a synagogue. Although not orthodox in practice, Ella's connection with Judaism is far from an apathetic one. She identifies strongly, through her family, her art and the Jewish Women's Group of which she is a member. We speak from the first floor of her home, overlooking leafy streets, and surrounded by photographs she has taken and cupboards containing many more.

It's interesting that a lot of people on all sides of my family had a lot to do with building the Jewish community here. My great-grandfather and his brother were cabinet makers and they helped build Bankstown Synagogue; Hannah Hart, my great-great-aunt, was First Secretary of the North Shore Synagogue; my grandmother's brother, Sam Karpin, was a founder of Wolper hospital; and my father was one of the founding parents at Masada College, and he's been President and Vice-President of the North Shore Synagogue, and he's there every week, twice a week.

It's funny because dad's family weren't religious in any way, certainly not in Germany. They were German Jews and not Jewish Germans. Dad said it was actually due to the Loreno home that Judaism was instilled in him. The family was able, through connections and paying for tickets, to get him and his brother on one of the ships and he was sent out here on a kindertransport, in 1939.

He lived at the Loreno home which the Jewish Welfare Society set up in Melbourne for the kids. It was run along reasonably religious lines and he was 12 when he got here so they gave him a bar mitzvah and he got involved with Judaism from then onwards and it stayed with him and grew. When I was growing up he was more inclined to live near the *shul* and was getting more and more religious. My mum had been a pretty assimilated Jew, it hadn't been her thing.

I became very religious in my teens. I had a great affiliation with the North Shore Synagogue. It was my home away from home. My grandmother and her friends used to call me 'the rabbi'. I went to synagogue a lot, I wouldn't travel on *Shabbat*, made a big fuss about who turned the lights on and off, used to pray a lot. It was a wonderful sense of identity, and belonging, and community. Even at *Habo* camp, where no one was particularly religious, I'd go off after dinner and sing *Birchat Hamazon* to myself. I became politically active too, going on big marches, demonstrating outside the Bolshoi Ballet outside the Regent Theatre when I was 14, marching up and down: 'Let my people go, save Soviet Jews.'

I went to my tenth year high school reunion ten years ago and a friend was saying to me 'Gee, I'll never forget you, you had such conviction, you were always on about Israel and Zionism.' And I was. It was my identity. And my family were always into it, Mum and Dad were always having *UIA* functions in the home and I always heard about Israel.

I went to Israel on *machon* after high school, the four of us did, my brother and two sisters. We loved it and were totally supported by my parents because they had a strong connection with Israel. But I got a huge shock in Israel: the reality of what Israel was. I honestly thought that when I landed — it was such an emotional landing for me, flying into Israel after my upbringing — that there would be dancing on the street like in the posters I'd looked at all my life. And I was really shattered. There were the guns, no one had prepared me for the social conflict, the fear. I went there with quite an open mind about the Arab–Israel conflict and after living there for a year I became terrified of Arabs. I also didn't know it was going to be a Third World as well as a First World country, I had just thought it was going to be clean and beautiful. It was really a shattering of dreams and beliefs and when I came back — I went there with *Habonim* and the idea was to come back and work in the movement — I couldn't continue. I spent a year in the movement and then left for good.

Plus the whole thing that no one in Israel was particularly observant was a real eye-opener. In my first couple of days there I was at someone's place for dinner and I said 'is this food kosher?' And they said 'no' and there I was, in Israel, what was I supposed to do now? I didn't know what to do. I ate the meat and that was the beginning of a lot of the undoing of my religious convictions. Israel had a big part to play in the undoing of my Jewish practice.

When I came back from Israel I didn't want to be religious any more. I gave a lot of it up and that was really hard. I still went to synagogue on *Rosh Hashana* and *Yom Kippur* because I was expected to but I deliberately went with old clothes and looked really daggy. I was just acting out something which now I understand: I was still in shock from my experience in Israel and was upset about it all, I hadn't worked out what was going on.

There was also another factor affecting me which was that I felt rejected by the institution for being a woman. Up to a certain age as a female in the *shul* you can run into the men's section and onto the *bimah* and everyone thinks it's cute. And when you get to another age you aren't welcome any more. Over the years that really took its toll on me.

At high school I met my first serious boyfriend. He wasn't Jewish and that was huge as I was quite religious at that time. He was an Australian boy from Newcastle and my dad went to pieces about it. But I was in love with him and wanted to be with him. When I went to Israel with *Habonim*, he came six months later and joined us on the kibbutz and was accepted by the group. We were together for seven years.

David, my husband, was born in Santiago and migrated from Chile when he was twelve. We also met in high school and had a secret passion for each other that lasted many years. His parents and my parents were friends from the synagogue. David had a non-Jewish girlfriend for five years as well but when he and I fell in love, it was very meaningful to us that we were both Jewish. I think in our early twenties when we lived with non-Jewish people we probably said it didn't really matter but actually it was part of the attraction, that he was Jewish, that there was an understanding of each other's cultural and historical background. But I certainly wasn't interested any longer in religious practice and either was David.

It's not that I walked away completely from anything Jewish. I've always had a practising Jewish family, which is nice and I feel very fortunate about that, and I still went home on *Shabbat* and festivals. But as my feminist consciousness grew, I just found it harder and harder to accept a lot of the rules and the behaviour of the tradition. I have had to find out where I belong and what's important to me.

David and I had a child together 10 years ago. When I was pregnant we were hit with what would we do about a *brit mila*. It was impossible to even have a discussion with either of our parents about should we or shouldn't we circumcise. We were in two minds, because we were not practising Jews, not religious. We also felt it was a horrible thing to do to a child, barbaric, and we struggled with that but luckily, we had girl. It would have been really hard for me to circumcise a child ten years ago but four years ago I had a boy, Axel, and it wasn't quite as hard to make a decision because during the six years since I had my daughter, I did come back to Judaism somewhat.

I sent my daughter, Felix, to local schools and then one Christmas she came home from school and said to me 'Mummy, I love the baby Jesus and Mary.' And David and I just looked at each other and thought, oh well, maybe it's time to do something about her Jewish education, and so she now goes to the Emanuel School. It was big decision for us, to send our daughter to a Jewish school.

I'm glad the Emanuel School exists. It's because there is equality between women and men there. It's somewhere she can go and have a Jewish education and have a sense that she has a right to be there. They have a religious service and I've watched the girls put on a *talit* and a *kippa* and everyone is having a turn and that feels so equal to me. She knows that she has a right to participate in Judaism as an equal member.

When Felix went to the Emanuel School, at age six, it was like she was putting on a cloak of identity. It was beautiful. She just flowered into this Jewish being and I was so happy that it meant so much to her.

I also have my Jewish Women's Group. It was started about seven years ago by women who had an interest in being Jewish but didn't want to belong to any of the institutions. It's a closed group, people can't just wander in and out and we don't advertise it. Most of us are about 40, a lot are working in the arts like I am. We have performers, film makers, visual artists, a social worker, lots of creative talent. And some of the people there I've grown up with, two I've known since kindergarten and *Habonim* days. We meet once a month for eating and drinking, discussion and workshops, writing and drawing, visualisation, dance, movement. We take turns in running our meetings, in having them in people's homes. We've got our own rituals which we've written and performed for each other. We've collected feminist *Hagadot* from Melbourne and America and have selected readings and constructed our own *Seder* incorporating traditional and modern elements and bringing women into the picture, acknowledging our presence.

The Jewish Women's Group has been fantastic. I feel like it's rekindled in me something very important, it's given me my own Jewish community. It's given me a lot of strength in being Jewish and I love the way we meet as Jews and as women, to support each other, to share experiences.

I think for a lot of us, when we were in our 20s, there were periods when we weren't terribly involved or interested in being active in Jewish life. For me, there were years when I went searching hard for spirituality. I went to Indian gurus, I went to Japan, to monasteries, did that classic search that ex-Catholics and Jews do. But in our 30s and 40s there is a growing sense of wanting to find some spiritual satisfaction in Judaism.

We have been quite affected by the many children of Holocaust survivors around the world who are making films and writing books. These things are really important to our group and we do a lot of reading, writing and film watching of works by other people our age, or maybe a bit older, who are addressing this. Most of the women in my group have stories, most are children of people who survived the Holocaust.

I have been to some services at the Temple Emanuel in Chatswood. Janece Cohen, the female cantor, is the drawcard. I was in the Temple two years ago and it was probably the first time I'd been there for a service. Seeing Janece up there on the *bimah* and seeing her little boy run up and jump on her back and muck around, hearing her sing — her musicality was phenomenal — I was crying. I went to my parents' home that day and I asked my father where I could get a *talit* from. He said, 'Would you like one? I'll give you one,' and he gave me a *talit* which meant so much to me because he knew I was going to wear it and he is an observant Jew. I went to the Temple on *Yom Kippur,* and I put it on and I was crying. For me to put on a *talit,* all my life it had been a taboo thing, never part of my experience as a Jew, and I loved wearing it. A girlfriend brought me a beautiful brightly coloured *talit* from Israel which I really treasure. Unfortunately Sydney's only female cantor and her rabbi husband have not had their contracts renewed. It's a great loss.

Apart from all that, I also belong to a spiritual group, which has nothing to do with anything Jewish. People from all backgrounds, all ages, all genders, meet along spiritual lines for spiritual reasons. When I was 28, I found this group and I felt I belonged from the minute I was there, because actually there is no dogma, you don't bow down to anyone. We just meet in old halls and community centres, because they're the cheapest halls to rent. We have meetings and we go away on weekend conventions. We have a singing group and I love singing. I taught the group two Hebrew songs. And, of course, I keep meeting other Jews there.

I've found that Judaism is coming out in my artwork more and more. Two years ago I was invited to give a guest lecture as an artist, which I do quite often, and it was the first time that I included images with a Jewish content. A lot of my main work has been about women, body image, sexuality, the female form, with a feminist consciousness, and now slowly this Jewish content is creeping out. It was fascinating. I felt that I was coming out in public as a Jew in my artwork. And my

Jewish Women's Group has had huge impact on that sense of confidence to be a visible Jew again in the world, because I was when I was young and then I wasn't for a long time and now I feel really comfortable again. My father gave me a large copper Star of David which I have started wearing out sometimes.

I have a project I want to do for my Master's degree. It will take me to Germany where I've been scared to go all my life. It's loosely titled *Beyond the Family Album* and I'm going to create and fictionalise my life as it were had my family not left Germany. I'm going to create a photographic family album of simulated family snapshots or portraits of a Jewish life that would or could have been were it not for the Holocaust. The artwork will be an act of reclamation of my lost heritage.

It's really important to me that my kids know they're Jewish and are exposed to Jewish culture and Jewish practice. I sing to them in Hebrew, we light the *Shabbat* candles, read Jewish stories and hold a wonderful *Channukah* party every year. I think they're getting the message.

The Newspaper Editor

Vic Alhadeff

The offices of the Australian Jewish News, of which Vic is editor, are situated in a large building known as the NSW Jewish War Memorial, home to many of the community's organisations. Upstairs is the Board of Deputies and State Zionist Council, below is the sheltered workshop and next door is the Sydney Jewish Museum. The weekly paper having gone to press the evening before, the office is relaxed. We sit in Vic's modest office surrounded by books and papers.

Both my parents were born on Rhodes Island, in Greece, which at the time was Italian. Their ancestors were expelled from Spain during the Spanish Inquisition and ended up on Rhodes, where they lived for many generations until 1944, when the Germans arrived. I have it on authority from the World Jewish Congress that it was specifically Kurt Waldheim who said that there was a Jewish community on Rhodes Island and something should be done about it.

My mother and her family had already left Rhodes for the Congo, as it was known then, on the last ship that was allowed to leave the island. My father was engaged to somebody, it's an interesting story. In 1938, Mussolini said Jews in Italy and Italian provinces could no longer go to schools and universities, so my father left for Southern Rhodesia. Other Jews from Rhodes had already gone there as it was a land of opportunity. He was hoping to send for his fiancée and his parents, but he wasn't able to. His parents were sent to Auschwitz and died there and both his sisters went, but survived. My father's fiancée also went to Auschwitz, and he thought she had died and she thought that he had died in the war, but 15 years ago he heard someone mention her name. He followed it up and discovered they were talking about the same person. She had survived the war and was living in Belgium. My father was in Europe a couple of years later and he looked her up; the last time he had seen her, they had been engaged to be married. It's an amazing story.

He and my mother married In Rhodesia. It was arranged by my mother's parents. My mother's father had been a rabbinical scholar and his word was absolute law and she would never dare disobey him. The marriage didn't work and they eventually divorced.

I grew up in Zimbabwe and went to university in South Africa. I started out doing law but then decided I wanted to do journalism so I completed a BA degree, did a teaching diploma in English and French and then went into newspapers.

I started at a newspaper called the *Diamond Fields Advertiser* in a small town called Kimberley and, after one year there, graduated to the *Cape Times,* which is Cape Town's major daily morning newspaper, where I became chief sub-editor. I was 29 at the time, the youngest chief sub-editor in the 100 year history of the newspaper. I remained there for seven years, when I was offered the position of editor of the *Zionist Record* which was one of three Jewish newspapers in Johannesburg. I remained there for three years and then went on *aliyah* with my wife, Nadene, and two-year-old daughter. We stayed in Israel for two-and-a-half years.

We loved being in Israel socially, and just the fact of being there. But I got enormously frustrated because of the language. While I could buy groceries in Hebrew, I found it impossible to be proficient enough in the language to be able to write or edit. I got a job as deputy editor of a magazine called *Newsview* and that position was perfect, exactly what I wanted. But three months later, the magazine folded.

Then I got a job as editor of the magazine of the South African Zionist Federation. It was not a challenging position, to say the least. Part of my job was carrying the 6,000 copies of the magazine on a trolley, through the streets of Tel Aviv to the post office. I got enormously frustrated.

In South Africa I'd written three non-fiction books on South African history, angled through newspapers — plus I had a successful career, and suddenly I was editing a newsletter. It was my push to go to Israel and it was my push to leave. I felt I had to get back into a country where I could function and operate in English.

But there was no question of us going back to South Africa. This was 1984 and Mandela was only released from prison in 1990, so it was still very much an apartheid society, and there was no way Nadene and I wanted to bring up children in a country in which there were four decades of legalised apartheid and 300 years of enshrined apartheid. There was no way we wanted to bring up children in a country where people were judged on the colour of their skin; where there was an entrenched belief system that if you were one colour you were superior to another colour; where there was ingrained racial tension.

A few years ago, I read Mandela's autobiography, *The Long Walk to Freedom*, about incidents that I lived through while working on the *Cape Times*. And the *Cape Times* was one of the most liberal newspapers and one of the most outspoken. Yet, even having witnessed those events from the perspective of a liberal journalist on a liberal newspaper, I was taken aback to compare my own relatively sheltered viewpoint in interpreting those events then, with Mandela's perspective. It was a society where racial prejudice was a part of the air you breathed.

So there was never any doubt, it was an absolute given, that we would leave once we married. Then it was a question of where to go and it was I who wanted to go to Israel. Nadene had spent a year in *WUJS* in the postgraduate program in Arad, so she was certainly partial to Israel. We had both been in Zionist youth movements as kids and it was very much part of our thinking, to give it a go. And I'm pleased we did, otherwise there would always have been a residual 'what if' sentiment.

After eighteen months, we returned to South Africa for a month, and by one of those bizarre quirks, while we were there, my brother-in-law happened to mention that sub-editors were on the list for Australia. I had been feeling enormously frustrated professionally, so the minute we got back to Israel I contacted the Australian Embassy and applied on that basis. We had bought an apartment in Ra'anana, which we sold, and five months later we were here. It was June 1986.

When I arrived in Sydney, I received four job offers within two days — essentially on the basis of having been chief sub-editor of the *Cape Times*. My preference was to join the *Australian Jewish News* because journalism is what I enjoy, but on the *Jewish News* it's not just another story, it's to do with issues that I care about. I joined as associate editor and, 10 years later, by February 1996, was appointed editor.

Settling in Australia, having previously migrated to Israel, was easy. Our daughters, Daniella and Michaela, were two years and six months old at the time, and we both have an attitude that you have to be positive, and go out and do it, and that there's no use sitting around and complaining. You just have to make things happen. We settled down very quickly and a thousand times over we are grateful that we were able to come to Australia. We love the lifestyle, the freedom, the acceptance of differences and of diversity. You can be who you are.

One thing that struck me when we arrived was the incredible support system that exists within the Jewish community. Particularly among the South African Jews on the North Shore, where we settled, there is an automatic support system where people know each other and speak the same language, loosely speaking, and have the same frame of reference.

This has led to criticism of the South African Jews, that they stick together and are a ghetto within a ghetto. This was the topic of a debate in which I took part at the *Hakoah* Club several years ago. There is a truth in that but there's also a reason for it and it's a function of any immigrant group. A friend of mine, a South African, walked into David Jones and the person who served him behind the counter was an Indian woman, also from South Africa; my friend asked her where she lived and she replied, 'In Campbelltown'; all the South Africans live in Campbelltown. I think that says a lot; settling in an area where there are numbers of expatriates is a comfort zone, and it feeds on itself.

Many South Africans have become involved in the Jewish community and have taken on a disproportionate number of positions of communal leadership. At the same time, there is also a substantial per centage who remain insular and don't get involved in wider issues beyond the kids' lunches and where the next holiday is and I certainly think that is a valid criticism. However, it is probably no more applicable to Southern Africans than it would be to any immigrant group.

Many South Africans arrive in Australia with almost a presupposition that this is still South Africa, with the same expectations and the same norms and same culture. While there are superficial similarities, there are enormous differences which often affect the way South Africans are perceived. Expressions like 'let me tell you' and 'you must do this' for example, even though the person may not be intending to be authoritative, create an impression of assumed superiority, which in turn elicits resentment among those already here. When I arrived I, too, was guilty of this. It takes a while for the edges to rub off. Yet a function of this assertiveness and aggressiveness is initiative and determination, and this has manifested itself communally and businesswise, with an inordinate number of business ventures being established by Jewish South Africans.

Communally, South Africans were very much pioneers of *Masada* College and the *Kehillat Masada* Synagogue. When we arrived, 12 years ago, there were 100 families at the synagogue; today there are 450, which is a phenomenal growth rate. When we arrived, you couldn't buy a *Rosh Hashana* card in St Ives, today there is a whole section in the Shopping Village saying 'Jewish cards', and that is obviously a function of the South African immigration of the last decade. There is a strong, flourishing and growing Jewish community on the North Shore. Ninety per cent of the *Kehillat Masada* community is South African, with a substantial segment comprising 'family reunion' immigration — people coming to the North Shore to reunite with family members who had immigrated previously.

Some people have relocated to the Eastern from the North Shore after achieving financial stability. But the numbers on the North Shore are still growing, due to new arrivals. Furthermore, parents wanting to send their children to a Jewish day school can do so with ease on the North Shore, as Masada has space.

A great deal of socialising occurs between Jewish kids on the North Shore and in the Eastern Suburbs. I think it is important, so that the North Shore kids do not live in an insular community, and also so that they and the Eastern Suburbs youth regard each other as all being part of the same community. This is important, especially in view of the barrier which is both created and represented by the Harbour Bridge for the older generations, both physically and psychologically, when it comes to social and cultural exchanges. The Internet has a lot to do with the change.

There are many members of the community from the Eastern Suburbs who never cross the bridge; at the same time, the majority of communal functions take place in the Eastern Suburbs, and there are many people on the North Shore who don't cross the harbour either physically or mentally, who could not tell you what the ECAJ is. That is why the seemingly increasing social interaction, within the university-age and high school-age generation, across the Bridge in both directions is a positive development, one which can only benefit both the individuals and the community as a whole.

My job here as editor of the only Jewish newspaper in the community is to provide a vehicle for Jewish community organisations, to give them a voice and to promote them. We also provide a forum, on our opinion pages and letters pages, for a robust and democratic exchange of views and ideas on a broad spectrum of issues. This is both healthy and important.

On another level, we are a newspaper and we cover whatever issues are happening, some of which may concern the same organisations which we are promoting. These two needs will occasionally conflict with each other, but it is essential for the ongoing well-being and development of the community that we continue to function as a vigorous and independent newspaper.

We regard ourselves as a newspaper with a communal responsibility, and from time to time, issues arise on which we feel we need to lead the community. A recent example was Aboriginal reconciliation. We've given this a great deal of publicity because it is a human rights issue and we feel it's something which the Jewish community, as Australians, should care about and get involved in and participate in, strongly and proactively. I once read a quote that the function of a newspaper is to 'comfort the afflicted and afflict the comforted' and I think that's an apt way of expressing it. I believe that no organisation is sacrosanct. There has to be accountability. And the *Australian Jewish News* doing its job properly helps to ensure this.

The *Australian Jewish News* is a human link in the community, from birth and marriage announcements to what's happening at all levels, whether it is racial vilification legislation or the impact of Pauline Hanson on the community. The other integral aspect of the paper is coverage of Israel. If Ethiopian Jews are unhappy in Israel or David Levy has a disagreement with Netanyahu, it might not make the dailies, so it's our task to bring our readers a perspective on Israel, to give them informed analysis and in-depth features and commentaries, not only on Israel, but on all matters of Jewish interest and concern.

There are also many issues which arise day to day. Recently, Rabbi Brian Fox went out on a limb, to his credit, saying he was prepared to talk to the *Beth Din* about having one standard of conversion, in an effort to resolve the deep divisions over this issue. Another issue which recurs is the Gay and Lesbian Mardi Gras. While some Orthodox rabbis, highly respected, prefer us not to write about this, as homosexuality contravenes *Halachah*, we are an inclusive newspaper. The Jewish gays and lesbians are saying, 'Let us in, we want to be part of the Jewish community.' If the establishment shuts them out, that's their decision, but that's not our role. We're inclusivist in that respect. Just last week we put together an investigative feature on being Jewish and gay, on the level of communal acceptance experienced by Jewish gays.

We frequently have two full pages of letters and that's wonderful. People care about the community and they care about issues. This is an exceptionally committed and active community, with many organisations and individuals, at all levels, from communal heads to youth leaders to school kids who are involved and who care about the Jewish community, to leaders of the world Jewish Congress and the Jewish Agency in Israel.

As to the future of the community, assimilation is certainly a reality, as it is in any Diaspora community. We often say we are ten years behind the United States and its 52 per cent intermarriage rate is often quoted here as a dire warning. I think that's disingenuous because the US doesn't have the Jewish day school system which we have, and that has to go a long way to countering a 52 per cent happening here.

I saw a wonderful T-shirt the other day, it said, 'Me paranoid? Who says I am?' I think that's part of the Jewish psyche, part of what makes Jewish people care. To have the history that Jewish people have and not to have an element of paranoia in us, to me that would be a worry. As Alan Dershowitz told me when he visited Sydney, Jews don't just look over their shoulder — they look over both shoulders!

I have dual roles in the community which complement each other. For my role as editor of the *Jewish News*, I need to take one step back to try to maintain a degree of objectivity and impartiality in relation to the organisations we write about. At the same time, I'm involved in the community personally. We have a daughter at Masada College, I coach a Northside Maccabi netball team, and I attend *Kehillat Masada* Synagogue. In addition, I give speeches for the Board of Deputies Speaker Service, both within the Jewish community and to the wider community as a form of outreach. I care deeply about Holocaust awareness and education, and have lectured in the Holocaust course run by the Comparative Genocide Studies Centre. All these activities, combined with my professional duties at the *Jewish News*, make for a gratifying whole.

In Search of Lost Tribes

Myer Samra

Myer greets me at the door to his home and guides me through the piles of boxes lining the hallway. They are filled with books donated by the Board of Jewish Education, en route to the Jewish community of India, Myer's area of academic interest and a personal passion. He is a lawyer and anthropologist specialising in the Sephardi community and the B'nai Menashe Jews of Northern India.

I was born in Baghdad, Iraq. As you know, Iraq today is the Babylon of the Bible, and there's been a Jewish presence there continuously from the time of Nebuchadnezzar's conquest of Jerusalem in 597 BCE until the present time. It's been a long and proud history; in fact, we were there twelve hundred years before the Arabs settled in Iraq. Some of the books of the Bible were written there, along with the Talmud. The sense of being connected with the very roots of Judaism was very strong among Iraqi Jews, with the reputed graves of the prophets Ezra and Ezekiel and Joshua the High Priest located in the country. These were important places of pilgrimage for the community over many centuries.

In modern times, the Jewish community in Iraq was perhaps the most advanced community in the country in many ways. The Jews were essentially the first to become Westernised, and they were pretty much a part of the fabric of the country. Baghdad itself was a predominantly Jewish city, until the early decades of this century. Sure, there had been anti-Semitism, but at the same time there was a sense of belonging, and prosperity. At the beginning of the century, Jews began moving out of their quarter, moving into the Christian Quarter of Baghdad, building finer, bigger houses, and moving into the suburbs. So they were fairly prominent, and many were prosperous.

In 1941 there was a pogrom of sorts. There had been a fair bit of propaganda in the country prior to the war, the German ambassador had been quite active, preaching anti-Semitism. During the war, a pro-Nazi group had staged a coup, expelled the royal family, and took control of the government. The British army marched back in to reclaim the country, beginning in Basra in the south and heading for Baghdad. They surrounded the city, but for symbolic reasons, didn't enter, until the Prince Regent could join them and lead the recapture. The first day of that siege, the Arab population inside Baghdad was tense, while the Jews were dressed up in their finery. It was the first day of *Shavuot*, but the mobs took them to be celebrating the arrival of the British troops, and so they attacked the Jews, a pogrom, in which a couple of hundred people were slaughtered. The British were outside and could see what was going on — and they didn't lift a finger. The second day, the rioters were followed by people who came from outside the city, just for the sake of looting Jewish property. This event shook the Jewish people, and a lot of them tried to leave the country after that. So while there's a sense of connection, a sense of history, a sense of belonging in Iraq, and the realisation that there had been hundreds of years of Jewish history in the one place, you also had at the same time a realisation that things had become quite dangerous.

After the State of Israel was established in 1948, the mobs were prevented from rioting by the imposition of martial law. As for the Jews, it was illegal for them to leave the country, though around 10,000 of them smuggled themselves across the border to Iran and then to Israel. In March 1950, the Government was disturbed by this illegal exodus and decided to give those Jews who wanted to leave twelve months to get out of the country. Not too many people left early in the year, partly out of suspicion about what the authorities might have planned, though nothing untoward happened to those leaving. Towards the end of the year, there was a big rush of people registering to leave, spurred on by things like a bomb that went off in the synagogue where people were registering. At the end of the twelve months, on a Saturday, Parliament held a secret session, without the knowledge of the Jewish Parliamentary members, and denaturalised everyone who had registered to leave the country, confiscating all their property. My father had pondered whether or not to leave and eventually chose not to. In a sense that was lucky in that we didn't lose all our property, and when we eventually left Iraq, we were able to do so with our passports, rather than as stateless persons.

Anyway, in 1950–51, the majority of the Iraqi Jews left the country. Israel took in about 120,000 people from Iraq in that one year. It would have been like the entire Jewish community in Australia packing up and saying good bye.

The people who remained behind, in the main, would have been people with property. My mother's family had been well-off merchants, and my father's uncle was the Chief Justice of the country, and one of his sons was a Member of Parliament. My father was an engineer. He'd studied in England and was working in the Irrigation Department.

I was a three-year-old when Dad decided we should leave Iraq, after the main Jewish community had done so, and we had a community of maybe 10,000 left behind with us. When he decided it was time to leave, Dad went off to England to look for work there. Dad later explained that he didn't feel we should go to Israel because the atmosphere would be just as tense as in Iraq. He would have to go into the army, and Mum would be left worrying about him, as well as about her three sons who would end up going into the army. So Dad thought it was better to go right away. He was offered a position in Australia, and was sponsored by people living there — in fact, by Rabbi Milecki's maternal grandfather, Yonah Joseph, whose brother was married to one of Mum's cousins. Most of our relatives had left to settle in Israel in 1950–51. By the time we left in 1956, only Dad's cousins stayed behind.

1969 was when most of the remaining Jews of Iraq felt they had better get out. When the Ba'ath Party seized power the year before, they arrested a dozen people, accusing them of being Zionists. At the time, Saddam Hussein wasn't the leader of the regime, but he was responsible for these arrests and the show trials which followed, leading to the public hanging of the accused. After that, Dad's cousins smuggled their families out of the country with the help of Kurds who got them across the border, leaving behind the palaces they'd built by the banks of the Tigris.

There are still about 100 Jews left in Iraq today. It'd been a wealthy community, and I guess the funds of the community would still be supporting the few people left, most of them now being quite elderly. I recall a small news item, about when the Iran–Iraq war began, Saddam Hussein called on all the women to help him with their gold for the war effort, and the Jewish women, being supposedly such great patriots, were the first to come forward with their jewellery.

Anyway, when we came to Australia, Dad got a job as an engineer with the Water Conservation and Irrigation Commission, and bought this house within a year, with funds they'd been able to get out of Iraq. My first school in Sydney was Bondi Public, in an infants' class. The teacher assigned one of the pupils in the class to look after me, and I happily followed her around until the scripture class came around, when they separated me from her, and told me I was 'Jewish'. Now I'd never heard that word before. I certainly knew I was a Yehudi, but I didn't know that I was Jewish, and I was scared about being sent out to this class in the lunch shed with an old woman, and separated from the one person I'd come to know in my class. I was crying and insisting I wasn't Jewish, but they still made me go. I feel so silly now remembering this — but when I got to the Scripture class, and the teacher was talking about Moses, and the stories seemed familiar, I settled down and felt okay, and learnt that here in Australia I was Jewish!

Mum was always a fervently religious woman, and our family was pretty strongly traditional and observant, though not quite in the way that we would call 'Orthodox' today. Dad's family had also been very religious when he was a child, but his faith was severely shaken when an older brother he admired dearly, who was very pious and very kindhearted, died suddenly when he was still quite young. After that, Dad just couldn't bring himself to sing the *pizmonim*, the Sabbath table songs which are a joyous part of Iraqi Jewish tradition. Also, living in England as an Iraqi student during the war, he wasn't too openly Jewish at all. Even so, when we were growing up, Dad was committed to a lot of Jewish tradition. We observed the Sabbath with *kiddush* on Friday night and Saturday morning, we were closely attached to the Sephardi Synagogue here, and we ate kosher meat. We didn't write on Sabbath or light the stove, though driving a car and switching on the electric lights seemed okay.

From the time I was a little child, they always told me I'd be a lawyer. I often heard the story about how Dad's uncle David, the great judge, was impressed with me and the way I argued as a kid, and said I'd make a good lawyer. At uni, I enrolled in Arts-Law, but I was more interested in my Arts subjects, and I had a degree of prejudice against the Law. I felt uncomfortable about making a living from other people's problems. So when I first completed my Law degree, I took a job with the Department of Youth, Ethnic and Community Affairs, and I guess I didn't expect it to become a long-term job, but I became quite enthusiastic about it. You're dealing with people's lives, seeing people's homes, people from everywhere and anywhere. As an Arabic speaker, I worked with lots of Lebanese families, and I felt a lot of tension about that and being a Jew, but that's another story in itself. After several years as a welfare worker, and feeling burnt out, I transferred into a legal position, and that's where my legal practice has been, with the Department of Community Services. I haven't got any interest in private practice. I can't see myself as a commercial lawyer, and really I don't have an interest in anything remotely commercial anyway.

In 1973 I went to Israel as a *mitnadev* after the Yom Kippur War. That was my first trip to Israel. I hated life on the kibbutz and escaped to my relatives every weekend. I've got hundreds of relatives in Israel, and I was getting to know them all for the first time. I came back to Australia very enthusiastic about Sephardi Jewry and wanted to do something for our Sephardi community here, to help it advance in some way. I joined the committee of the NSW Association of Sephardim and wrote a couple of articles, kind of like rallying calls.

And I also began studying the community, the people, where they came from, what they were doing, how they were fitting into

Australian society. I did my PhD on the Sephardi community. It was a study of Jews of Iraqi background in Australia, and I'm proud of the praise I've received for it. I completed the study on a part-time basis, while I was working at the same time. I guess I probably would never have finished it until Mum died in 1985, and my big brother Eli decided to make sure I did finish it, as a kind of tribute to her. He gave me a dictaphone and got me dictating, and he'd ring me up to find out how much I'd done each day. And I felt bad unless I could tell him I'd finished a mini cassette in a day. That's the way I did the first draft.

The history of Iraqi Jewry and Indian Jewry overlap quite a bit, and I guess in some ways I have always had a degree of identification with things Indian. Mum, when she'd gone on a trip to Israel in 1966, stopped off in Bombay, and came back with a small booklet on the Jews of India, and the fact that there were three separate Jewish communities there fascinated me. I read whatever books I could find, anything on the B'nai Yisrael, anything on the Cochin Jews or the Baghdadi Jews in India. Also, as a vegetarian, on my first trip overseas I wanted to go to India. Vegetarianism was a big part of my philosophical world. In primary school I was preaching vegetarianism in class, but at home I wasn't allowed to be vegetarian, even though it had always distressed me that people were killing for food. That had a big influence on my emotional state, and I finally refused all meat at the age of fifteen.

My interest in the B'nai Menashe community goes back to 1988, when there was a letter received by the Executive Council of Australian Jewry, from a man calling himself Yechiel Sharon Bene-Israel B'nai Menashe, from a place called Moreh in Manipur, North East India, asking for help with prayer books and *talitot* and *tefilin* and *mezuzot*, saying 'We live in an isolated part of India and we want to pass on our traditions to our children, but we're afraid we haven't got the resources.' That letter intrigued me, and I was interested in following it up.

A year earlier, Mizoram, next door to Manipur, had achieved statehood, and for the first time foreign journalists entered the territory. Many of their stories picked up on the fact there were Jewish people here, and they were having problems. I put up the subject of these Jews as a research project for a Golda Meir Post-Doctoral Fellowship at the Hebrew University, and once it was accepted I began going off to India, as well as meeting the first batch of twelve young people from Manipur and Mizoram who came to Israel in November 1989.

On my first trip to India in 1990, I wasn't able to get into the North East, but I met some of the people from there who were in Bombay studying, and attending the synagogue. I was lucky to make it into Manipur later in the year and wrote an article which was published in the journal *Man in India*. In 1992, I was invited to an International Seminar in Mizoram, and that was an incredible experience for me. I had written a paper on Judaism in North East India for the Seminar, so my visit to Mizoram had already made it into the press before I'd arrived.

There's a very strong identification with Israel there, people who feel very close to the country. When Israel was at war, one man recorded everything broadcast on the BBC, translating it all for people to follow. My attendance at the Seminar got quite a lot of attention, and I had quite a big following. Locals, who didn't speak English, were coming to the conference just to look at me. Everywhere I stayed, people were banking up at seven in the morning to speak to me.

One person coming to see me was a woman, a visionary from Burma. She apparently had a vision that she was to see an Israelite in Mizoram in April of that year, so she trekked for three days to Champai on the border, and rode one more day in a truck to Aizawl, the capital of Mizoram. I was there when she arrived, and she was keen to see me. She told me how she'd fallen while cultivating the side of a hill many years ago, and fell into a coma. And when she eventually came to, she began to hear voices telling her things, and that was what led her to come looking for me. I thought she'd come to me to heal her, so I put my hands on her head and pronounced the blessing of the *Cohanim*, but as it turned out, that wasn't what she'd come for. She had a vision she wanted to relay, and that was that the area inhabited by the Chikim should be neither part of India nor Burma but should be in union with Israel, an eastern territory of

Israel, and people would come from Israel to mine for gold in the hills here. And from that gold, they would mint coins with the image of the Messiah — and that was the vision she was passing on to me.

People in this region who are practising Judaism today had previously been practising a mixture of Jewish and Christian traditions before they adopted Judaism and gradually distanced themselves from Christianity. A large part of it came from reading the Bible and taking the words of the Bible literally. They identified with the Israelites in the Bible, believing that their ancestors had been Israelites. You can't help admiring them, for they taught themselves about Judaism, before finally making contact in 1975 with Jews in Bombay.

I went to Israel again in 1994 to follow up what was happening with the people from India who were settling there, all of them entering with assistance from Rabbi Avichail and his Amishav organisation. After the first batch in 1989, more young people came in 1991, then, in 1993, another group of around 40 came. In 1994, the Israeli Government had agreed to take in another hundred people, and Rabbi Avichail had already selected the people who were to come.

Unfortunately, only half had arrived in Israel when the Israeli Ambassador in India sent a cable to his Minister, expressing concern that if we allow people into Israel as members of the Lost Tribes, there could be as many as 300,000,000 Indians who might make the claim to try and come. That kind of changed the attitude to these people. Whereas the press and the general public in Israel had been showing them goodwill, seeing them as interesting and exciting, now they were suspicious. Instead of seeing the Bene Menashe as they were, as practising Jews, people worried whether they were the vanguard of millions of imposters trying to leave the misery of India for a life of affluence in Israel. And the official attitude to the Bene Menashe changed, for all this caused the visas for those who hadn't yet arrived to be frozen. So I got involved on behalf of these people, writing articles and submissions, stressing the fact that these are people living and practising Judaism. I was doing a bit of advocacy work for them.

Unfortunately, around October 1994, Malka, the youngest girl who'd arrived the previous year committed suicide. Most of the people who'd come with her had already successfully undergone *giyur*, and she was embarrassed that she hadn't as yet. But it was through this tragedy that I came to be involved with Miriam, that's when I really came to know her. I must confess that I'd already taken an interest in her before that. I liked what I'd seen of her. She was a teacher, and she took on a lot of responsibility for members of the community. She was taking people to the Ministry of the Interior to sort out their papers, and she seemed to spend a lot of her time helping quite a few different people, from both Manipur and Mizoram, and that was something I found quite attractive.

The first time I tried to speak to her, Miriam deflected my advances. Miriam makes fantastic crocheted *kippot*, and I tried to commission her to make one for me, but she wasn't interested. After Malka died, Miriam and I were both working to help the members of the group, who were still feeling pretty vulnerable in Israel, through their grief. Here, Miriam appreciated the role I was playing, and she allowed herself to show an interest in me.

We decided to get married in 1995, and Miriam insisted that I write to her father in Manipur to ask his permission. I felt embarrassed about doing that — it's not something I'd done before, writing to tell someone that I wanted to marry his daughter, and it wasn't easy. Apparently, Miriam's father was unhappy at first about this man from Australia writing to him, but members of the community who knew me reassured him that I was okay, and I got back a hand-written letter, in beautiful copperplate script, expressing pleasure and delight at my proposal, with praise to *Hashem*.

We got married in March 1996, and I'm proud to say that Miriam presented me with probably her finest crocheted *kippa*, exquisitely replicating the patterns on one of the traditional designs woven on shawls in Manipur. Miriam's made me several other *kippot* since, but this one I treasure the most.

After the wedding, we stayed on in Israel for a couple of months, and then spent a couple of months in India, when I met her family for the first time. Since then, we've been back in Australia, and Suzette, our lovely daughter, was born here.

Converting Gay

Michael Nisner

Michael is one of very few actively identifying gay and lesbian Jews in the community. Complicating his story is his arrival at Judaism through choice, having converted from Christianity, rather than from birth. He has become a spokesperson for gay people and an active member of the Reform Temple, where he has found a welcoming home. I arrive at Michael's apartment to find him doing his finances.

I came to Judaism through choice, I was not born Jewish. I grew up in the Christian religion and found that in my teens and 20s I wandered from church to church because I was not happy in the church I was in and assumed it was something in the dogma of each of the different denominations.

I ended up with Catholicism and started teaching in the Marist Brothers and something I was actually going to do down the track was join the brotherhood because I always had a strong sense of spirituality, connection to God. But I was still very confused with what I was doing because teaching religion I remember the number of times I had my knuckles rapped for teaching from the Jewish Scripture and not the Christian ones.

They said go away for a while and have some time in Rome. So I stayed in a nunnery of all places and spent some time meeting people in the Vatican. My trip to Europe started really making me see the problem with Christianity and that was because it was idolatry, I couldn't see the connection to God.

Somehow or other, fate, God leading me, I ended up in Israel.
And as soon as I stepped off the plane that was it, I knew I was home.
I started having my first contact with Jewish people, Jewish lifestyle
and when I came home I started looking into what Judaism was.

Then a friend of my mum's, he's an American Jew, was coming to
Australia and he rang and asked if I would find him a liberal *shul*
because he had *yahrtzeit* coming up. So I picked him up from the
airport and he took me to *shul*. It was the first time I actually went to
a full service and from there, that was it.

I then made the conversion and I started living at the Reform
synagogue really. I attended everything that was available whether it
was a service, a course or a lecture or function. At the same time I
kept a very open mind because at that stage I well and truly
understood the differences between the interpretation of Judaism
from Reform and Orthodox, so I didn't shut the door on anything
and I started formulating what Judaism was from my point of view.

When it was time to make that serious decision whether I was
progressive or Orthodox I started realising there were too many
things in the Torah which to me represented history. I had a problem
with a lot of the issues so therefore had to look at Judaism from a
progressive point of view, that it is God-inspired. I think a lot of
Torah may be God-given but there is a lot of it fluffed up with man's
history in there too. I think the Torah has to be lived for the day we
are living in, it has to be adaptable and vibrant and alive for the
community and generation that we are practising in. One example is
that I started keeping *shabbat*. I'm not *shomrei shabbat*, that's for sure,
but I do try and keep it in as many ways as possible but I do very
openly state I drive on *Shabbat*. I don't get in my car and drive for a
picnic somewhere but for me to get from here to my synagogue, for
me to keep *Shabbat*, I have to drive.

My family were very supportive of my decision. Dad's never been
that interested in any of the religious part of my life so it was just a
case of ho hum that's wonderful. He's been to Sydney but he's never
come to *shul* with me or he's never really even asked what it is. Mum
is very much involved with everything I do so if she comes to Sydney
during a festival she participates in it. If she's here on Friday night

she'll come to *shul* with me. She probably took about a year or so to understand it.

When I first told my dad I was gay, I was in my early 20s, he had a big problem with it. He went very quiet for the first day or so and then started the usual pattern of blaming himself, then the next step which is usually, 'Why have I done it to him,' then to, 'I don't want to know anything about you, don't you dare bring your friends into this house,' which went on for quite a while. My father's family is Yugoslav so it was a very traditional kind of thing, he was the head of the house and everyone did as he said and of course to be gay was definitely not what he said so therefore I was a threat to his authority in the house. Eventually I said fine you don't want my friends in my house so fine you don't want me in the house. That went on for about two years until he finally said would you like to bring Bradley home. The breakthough happened there.

Mum on the other hand was very supportive but understood nothing about being gay. She didn't know how to handle it because she wanted to be supportive of me but she did the right thing and went out there and read, saw the doctor, got some ideas.

I think a lot of guys don't come out whether Jewish or not because you're protecting the family. I've now got to say protecting them from what. In the meantime all you're doing is persecuting and torturing yourself. This will keep going on until you basically say I've had enough and I can't protect the family anymore. So I did it. I just came out in one full swing. I've never had a problem with being gay and if the question was posed to me even as a 15- or 16-year-old: would I take that magical pill to make me straight, the answer is no, I wouldn't. Even then I wouldn't have.

Aleph was started as an organisation to be plonked right in the middle of the Jewish community. There's always been several gay groups for Jewish people but Aleph wanted to be a gay Jewish group. The issue needed to be addressed in the Jewish community. It was addressed everywhere else and the Jewish community had not caught up. What I was finding about being gay and Jewish was that the Jewish community was actually ready. Aleph came along at the right moment. The worst I can say is I've had a couple of rolled eyebrows from people when they realised I was gay or when I've heard rabbis discuss gay issues from the pulpit. There are only one or two very ultra-Orthodox rabbis here in Sydney who have got a very big problem with the gay issue and one rabbi specifically who even targeted me and Aleph in a *Yom Kippur* service about how dare they set up a violators' organisation in Judaism.

The Orthodox, to a certain extent, have painted themselves into a corner on quite a few issues. One being homosexuality. I have to admit when I first came to the concept of Aleph and gay and lesbian issues within the Jewish community, I was stupid enough to believe the *halacha* would be circumvented, re-written, re-worded, that there was going to be some change coming in some way that that law would no longer be there. The prohibition on homosexual acts is of course one of the 613 laws in Judaism. I understand now that that could never happen, there is no way it can. I've now started to understand and believe that law has to stay, you can't change it. Some of my friends say why don't we go around and get rid of the law completely. I would have big problems going around to every Torah scroll with a piece of white ink and blocking it out. I don't want to do that, it is part of our history and I have to respect that. But it is not applicable to my generation nowadays.

To a certain extent, Orthodox Judaism almost takes a Christian way around something: love the person, hate the sin. If I choose to live an Orthodox life, they would accept me as an Orthodox Jew if I made a statement that said I do not practise my homosexuality. I'm not going to lie about my lifestyle. To me, that is defeating the purpose of Judaism, to lie, and progressive Judaism gives me the freedom to be who I am.

Aleph has been quite successful as an educational tool in the Jewish community just by its existence. I've been invited to quite a few different areas to talk. It's been good to present three or four people who are gay and Jewish within the community and break some of the stereotyping. There is a mailing list of over 400 gay and lesbian Jews in Sydney alone and that is still only a scratch in the iceberg.

It was there as a chat line for Jewish people to ring up and have a chat. Strangely enough, I also get a lot of phone calls from gay

Muslims. I ask them after a while why don't you get in touch with the Anglican Church or Catholics and they say, 'Oh, no, our religions, we're brothers.' If anyone rings up, I try and ask where they are in their lives, what's going on and either know they're coming to terms and just want a talk and get ideas or if I feel there are problems developing and a crisis I've got a series of councillors so I can say, 'Why don't you give such and such a ring?'

I think half the group is quite comfortable being gay but no one knows they are gay. Some would be living outwardly heterosexual lifestyles because they've never been challenged about it. A friend of mine, for example, he's a *Masada* boy, most people just think he's heterosexual and in no way did he ever correct that thinking until recently. Now that he's started correcting people he's found interesting results because he's finding people aren't rejecting him, they're more or less saying, 'I never knew that,' that type of attitude. I haven't yet spoken to a gay Jew who has said, 'I told friends or family and I've been rejected.' I do have one example where the child did come out to his mother and she said, 'Why did you tell me that, why didn't you tell me you had cancer or something like that.' That's the only example I ever heard and that story is going back 15 or 20 years. The other half is gay in their identity and they are not sure if they have any connection with the Jewish community.

I'd well and truly like to have a Jewish partner. I believe in keeping our traditions alive and I'd like to run a Jewish household. I live a Jewish lifestyle and I'd like a Jewish partner to share it with. There have been several gay Jews that I have met and we have gone out and stuff like that and usually after a week or so of involvement the other person freaks, gets very cold feet, because the moment they're seen with me they'll automatically be outed because of my role in Aleph.

During one of my discussion nights in the synagogue a couple of people said to me why don't you have a family and I said I'd like to and explained to them my situation at the moment that I feel too old and I'd have a double generation gap by the time my kid was a teenager. I said to them I've done a lot of work in the Jewish community and I just don't know if the Jewish community yet is ready to have a gay person having a family. I actually had my head ripped off for that one. They came back quite severely and attacked me, and said that's wrong, how dare you think like that, you must realise that if you are bringing up a Jewish child you are part of the community. So maybe the Jewish community would support a gay household.

The *Jewish News* rings me up two weeks before Mardi Gras every year to ask if we'll have a float in it. I would like to do something in the Mardi Gras. It has a lot of good stuff that is very political, very statement-oriented. But there is also a large amount of it that so far over the top that it then gives the stigma that everybody is like that. It creates a whole concept that gay men throw on frocks all the time. And there's no way I want to feed homophobes in our community, 'See, I told you that's what they're like.'

The Orthodox Jewish Teacher

Peta Jones Pellach

Peta's office is in the Jewish residential college at the university. She is one of the few home-grown professional Orthodox Jewish educators, most in the community having been employed from overseas. She is also a member of the Jones family, renowned for its active involvement in communal life. With coffee in hand, we head for the college library.

One of the strong influences in our lives is that we were never affluent. My parents had very strong values and made us feel we were well-off because we had these values and emphasised these above possessions. It was snobbery misplaced, if you like. We knew our family grew up with something very important that we knew not everyone else had. So much of our lives, when you analysed it objectively, was to do with lack of affluence.

The five of us, we've all made our own decisions. Nobody has abandoned Judaism. Far from it. We're all very involved, but in different ways. Quentin went on *aliyah* a few years ago and we're very proud of his decision. Jeremy is the face of the Sydney Jewish community to the outside world. He's able to work out the best way for the Jewish community to be portrayed. He's not in the least bit spiritual, but he's sent his kids to Jewish day schools and he goes to *shul* regularly. My sister Melinda is a lecturer in law at the university. Her main areas of work involve disability and rights, rights of the child in particular. She's proud to say this is part of her Jewishness and she's made sure her children have a strong Jewish education.

Amanda is a clinical psychologist and she often proclaims her Jewishness publicly, even when it's not to her best advantage. We were listening to her on the radio yesterday and she was saying '... in my Jewish tradition ...' So all my family are very proud to proclaim who they are. It's interesting to see our children; we see all of them are very strong Jews, they know who they are.

The first real push for us all was *Habonim*. We loved it, we were devotees from the moment we hit it. All through my school years, life consisted of *Habonim* and if you could fit school around it that was OK.

We girls were aware that when we turned 12, we were bat mitzvah; that there was a change of life, a rite of passage. It was different now. You had to fast on *Yom Kippur*, you made the choice. I knew that from the time I was 12 the choices I made were mine and I was responsible for them.

So I started going three times a week to Hillel Academy, by public transport. It took an hour and a half each way. My teacher was Eddie Pilcer, master teacher of Sydney. He loved the *Tenach*, he loved the language. He was marvellous and nurturing and a strong influence on anyone who wanted to learn and so it was worth persisting.

Always with my Jewish growth it's been family first and theology has followed behind. When we had Friday night at home it was a beautiful but intimidating experience. My father used to sit at the head of the table and quiz us on intellectual, political or communal issues and we were expected to be on the ball, forming opinions, and were expected to defend those opinions. The intellectual stimulation at the table was a part of the family culture. You had to be on top of it and with it and to defend your view, remembering to be deferential to my father because, after all, he was head of the household.

In those days, in Sydney, no one wore outwardly Jewish symbols. Even the Orthodox rabbis didn't wear *kippot* in the street, they wore hats. If you wore a *magen david* it was very little. You weren't flamboyant about your Judaism. That was one thing about our family: we were often in the spotlight as the Jewish family. So when the ABC wanted to do something about *Pesach*, they filmed our family. We were known as Jewish.

After I finished school I spent a year in Israel. We had a trip to Haifa and I looked at the street and realised you couldn't tell the Jews from the Arabs and that was a watershed moment in my life. It started me wanting to seek more outward expressions of Judaism.

I was a proud Australian but what was making me, a Jewish Australian, different from a non-Jewish Australian? I thought it was important to have living cultural expressions of my Jewishness. When I returned I was more determined then ever to integrate my religion with my activity in *Habonim*. I was very active and very devoted and a lot of it had to do with setting myself apart from my peers.

We always kept kosher at home. My mother's line was, 'so that any Jew can eat in our home' but I became much stricter than my parents about *kashrut*. I was constantly forced to balance my own religious principles and I decided my respect for my parents was more important then my particular level of *kashrut*. Things that I wouldn't do in other people's houses I would do in my parents' house, and that was a religious decision.

As far as actually hearing God's voice, feeling communicated with, I never had an experience or a moment. But I do have a strong sense that our history and our survival are miraculous, are supernatural, and I feel a strong sense of obligation to maintain this link.

I don't grapple with God on a daily basis, it's not my thing. I have the belief that God exists and that God wants something from us. But I don't believe there's an immediate reward for good deeds. I believe in the Talmudic dictum: He's good and bad things happen to him and he's bad and good things happen to him', that's the reality of life and I get very nervous about the missionary zeal of some Jews: 'Do *mitzvahs* and your life will be better.' There are certain ways of living Orthodox Judaism that do enhance family life but it's not because they offer a miraculous cure; it's a whole package.

I believe some of the issues of the rights of women, or lack of them, in Jewish life, are not to do with God at all. They are a perversion, particularly what happened with the *gett* and the *aguna*, the woman who finds herself unable to remarry. I don't see that as God's will. Women were non-issues or non-entities for so many of our rabbinic authorities for so many generations, so certainly there are glaring omissions that are not within the spirit of the Torah. But the vast majority of decisions on how to live a Jewish life according to *halacha* is healthy, enriching and something that gives us a sense of tradition.

I got into Arts-Law at university and was thinking of it in terms of ethics, and I hated it, I saw it as torts and contracts. I was more attracted to the student campaigns and the work with *AUJS* and I virtually took my BA and ran when I had the opportunity to not finish law. Then I was left without the qualification to do anything and at that time Arthur Hertzberg came here to advise the community on the Palestinian campaign and he met with the students. He asked what I was doing and I said I was going on *aliyah* and he said, 'You have to come and get a Master's first. Come to Columbia University, New York. America was the enemy because of the Vietnam War, America was the baddy and it never occurred to me to go there. In short that's how I ended up doing my Master's at Columbia in International Affairs which I loved. I loved the intellectual stimulation. It was the first time that I found what grappling on an intellectual level could really be, in an academic environment. Being at Columbia and being in New York was really being in the world. I met Jewish people there from all streams. I met women who were involved in women's *t'fillah*. I saw women reading from the Torah. These were women who were grappling for recognition within Orthodoxy and it was awe-inspiring. Young people trying to investigate and explore Jewish issues together. I was so impressed with people who were on that search.

In New York I met my husband, at Israeli folk dancing. He said 'Can I drive you home?' I said, 'Great, and if there's parking do you want to come up for coffee?' and he's always joked that he'd said OK with absolute certainty there would be no parking. There's never any parking. But we got to my building and there was a parking spot right outside and we always said that's God's intervention in our lives. Somehow an Israeli and an Australian met in New York and we knew immediately we were going to marry each other. We came here to Australia for two weeks in August to get married. I finished my Master's in May, had my baby in July and we came back to Australia for a visit in December and are still here.

I got a maternity position with the Schools' Commission, dealing with The Innovations Program, looking at projects in schools and funding them and it was very exciting. Then I tutored at Macquarie University for a year. By then my oldest daughter was starting pre-school and I walked up the road to the Jewish school and said 'Are you interested in me doing any teaching'. So they said 'We'd like you to teach the bar mitzvah class', and I must say to you in the years I taught them I was constantly striving to do something meaningful for the girls. I was very conscious young girls growing up were going to need expressions of their Judaism which perhaps my family and *Habonim* provided for me. Most of the children did not come from homes which were supportive of the ethos of the school at all, on the contrary, some were undermining, so every minor success was a major success and every child that was actively Jewish, you felt you had done something important.

In 1988, I saw an advertisement for a program called the Jerusalem Fellows. It was an opportunity for my whole family to go to Israel for two years. Those two years in Jerusalem really changed our lives. Aharon re-found spirituality and I guess mine was strengthened too. We met people who inspired us and we were in an environment that was conducive to spiritual growth and the main influence in my life, the teacher of Torah, Nechama Leibowitz, came then. Many of the things I was doing for cultural or historical or communal reasons really did take on a spiritual dimension which hadn't been there before.

When I came back, I started working with the Melton program for adult Jewish education and it's overtaken me. It's the most inspiring thing to see that this year we have over 300 people coming once a week to learn about their Jewish roots and their heritage and they're from all walks of life and all belief systems, and they want to know. I've had the opportunity to learn from great teachers starting from my parents and it's now an opportunity to pass some of that on to people who are hungry for it, who want to learn. However, I don't think Melton is the be-all and end-all of Jewish learning, our community needs a lot more.

I do believe education is a key to continuity but it's not the only key. Knowledge is an enabler but it's not the issue. I think with regards to continuity, people have to feel what they're doing is important enough to hand on. The way I see it, the general despondency with values in Australia is making people want to seek values, and Judaism has them. The problem is that our leadership doesn't espouse values and people aren't going to want to be in the Jewish community simply because it's well run. People will want to belong if it offers some values they are seeking. If our lay and professional leadership become more knowledgeable and see the values in Judaism and is not scared to articulate them, then we may be heading in a healthy direction. If on the other hand, they see their professional roles somehow separate from Judaism, then we're in trouble. This has no longevity. The key to our survival is a community that stands for something, has some values to which children can aspire. I've got hope, I'm an eternal optimist.

Alan Dershowitz said something significant to me. He said it's never amazing to him when a Jew marries out in America. What amazes him is when Jews marry each other, because we don't give them enough common ground to feel we belong together. If families don't give their children enough of a feeling that being Jewish is intrinsic to who they are, then why should they want to bother with another Jew?

VOICES FROM THE NEW GENERATION: 1960s AND BEYOND

Finding the Middle Ground

Tmne Blair

Two of Tmne's siblings are ultra-Orthodox and two are married to non-Jewish spouses. She has found the middle ground. I meet with Tmne in the two-bedroom Bondi flat she shares with her husband of one year, David. He has left to go to the beach and we relax into the leather couches.

In one sense my immediate family is in itself a real cross-section of the Jewish community, from fully assimilated to ultra-Orthodox, and I guess I'm in the middle.

I have three brothers and a sister and we grew up in Drummoyne, which is by no means a Jewish suburb. The first time I remember thinking I was different was in third grade at the school tuck shop. I saw an advertisement for these new chips: Bacon Rings. I was eating them while I was with my brother, waiting for our piano lessons to start after school, and he looked at me and said: 'We don't eat that, we're Jewish.' And I've never eaten them since, they didn't taste very nice.

But it wasn't really until high school that I really thought about being Jewish. I suppose that came about because my brother, who is immediately older than me, started studying for his *bar mitzvah* and becoming religiously much more observant. He slowly built up his practices. He wore *tztitzit*; started laying *tefilin*; started going to *shul* every day. He was learning Hebrew and decided not to travel on *Shabbat*.

When I was in Year 10 he went to America to do his last year of high school on an exchange program and he lived with a non-Jewish family and somehow he managed to keep kosher there. But then, when he was coming home, he said, 'I've lived for a year with a family that's not my own and not even Jewish and I managed to keep kosher and I'd really like to keep kosher in my own home.' By that stage it had been quite a few years and my parents knew it wasn't a passing fad so we decided to make the whole house kosher for his return. Since then he's now moved countries and rarely comes home but my parents still have a kosher home.

Just before he went to Israel he became engaged to his girlfriend who he'd been going out with for about three years. He met her because he used to walk to synagogue every Saturday morning. From Drummoyne to the City was about an hour and three-quarter walk, through an industrial area. To save him the walk back, her father, the Rabbi, used to invite him every Saturday back to his place and then my parents would go after sunset to pick him up. I assume that became the basis for their courting. They emigrated to Israel about eight years ago, and he's been studying at a yeshiva and teaching there ever since.

His religious outlook on life has influenced the rest of his family and made us think about our culture and who we are. Most immediately it's affected the two siblings closest to him in age. Both of us dabbled in keeping Orthodox laws — my middle brother with more success than me, I suppose. He also went to Israel, where he worked on a religious kibbutz and became religious. I really can't comment on the path he took to becoming religious, because most of it happened while he was away. He went away the slob that we all knew and came back a different person. He now lives in Israel and is married to a very religious South African woman and they have three children.

My sister was the first of us to move out of home and get married. At the time it was more of a controversy that she moved out of home to start with, and then that she moved out of home to live with a boy, that we didn't give much thought to the fact that he wasn't Jewish. When my sister decided to get married, my parents couldn't turn around and say 'you're not allowed to marry a non-Jewish boy.' Because they didn't do the work. They never encouraged her to mix with Jewish boys. They never gave her the lifstyle where that's something important, so they couldn't suddenly turn around and say they're not happy about it.

My eldest brother started going out with a nice Jewish girl and it looked like it was going swimmingly and they had a nice crowd of friends and they got engaged and it looked like it was going well. But obviously it wasn't, because my brother wasn't happy, and one way or another the engagement broke off and my brother started going out with another girl and they've been living together now for ten years.

My parents, for all their faults, their one great triumph is that they don't have a single set of rules that they apply in all situations. They look at each individual situation and each individual that it affects. So, when a decade later I was going out with a non-Jewish boy and it looked like we might get married my parents did turn around to me and say we'd support you if you did this but we don't think it would make you happy, because we think your Jewish lifestyle is very important to you.

I think I became religious more out of respect for my brother rather than from an understanding of what I was doing. I could see that he was very happy on a very basic level and I thought it could make me happy too but it didn't. I found the rules were much more of a burden than a release, whereas my brother seems to enjoy the structure of his lifestyle. I found it very suffocating and I wasn't enjoying it. Slowly I stopped them one by one and every one that I stopped seemed to lift the load off my shoulders a little bit more. So now I feel that I'm at a stage with my religion that I'm very comfortable. It's a personal thing where I do the observances that I like, that I find meaningful, and I don't do the things that I find ludicrous.

At the moment David and I are looking for a permanent synagogue to go to. Since our wedding I found that I want a *shul* which caters more for a young couple looking towards being a young family than the Great Synagogue does. We'll probably have a few more years of dithering around the various overflow services until we park ourselves at a synagogue.

If I had children ready now for school age I wouldn't send them to a Jewish school, because we couldn't afford it. I would prefer to because, of my cousins, brothers and sisters, only one went to a Jewish school and the fact that he knows Hebrew alone is worth it. It seems bizarre, but since my grandfather died and my brothers went to Israel, my little cousin, he's not so little, he's now 18, is in charge of leading our *seder* nights because he's the only one who can read the *Haggada*.

It would bother my husband greatly if our children didn't marry Jews. I would like to think that we'll give our children a good upbringing so that that actually never becomes an option. I don't want my children to feel that being Jewish is a burden. I want them to feel it's a bonus. But if by some fate they fell in love with someone who wasn't Jewish and that was their path, I would have to respect that.

Thinking about this reminds me of how once, when I was visiting Israel and it was a *Shabbat* afternoon, I went out for a walk with my sister-in-law and somehow we got around to this kind of conversation. She said to me, and this was from her perspective of growing up in an Orthodox family, that she thought it was a bit of a failure in my parents that out of five children only two became very religious and one moderately so, and that two, in her classification, were failures. I was very upset with her and I said: 'On the contrary, it's a triumph of the way my parents brought us up that two people in my family actually managed to become religious when all the odds were pitted against it.' My parents could see so far into the future that the things they were allowing my brothers to do went against almost everything they were brought up doing, and everything they actually brought us up to do. I think that's been a real triumph in our family.

Growing up Lubavtich

Yosef Feldman

I meet with Yosef, or Yossi, in the Synagogue of the Yeshiva learning centre where he is the midst of a discussion with a visiting South African Rabbi. In his late–20s, he is bearded and dressed in a traditional black suit with his black hat lying beside him. This young rabbi's life experience has been with the ultra-Orthodox Lubavitch movement, which his father heads in Sydney. Throughout the interview, we are interrupted by rabbinical students carrying large texts in Hebrew and Aramaic, seeking clarification of a difficult part of the Jewish text they are studying.

When I grew up, there weren't too many religious families living in Sydney, especially with children my age. In my class at school, there were maybe one or two other observant students, and even they were not on the same level in their *Yiddishkeit*. I was quite lonely in the sense that I lived my own life, in my own way, and the other kids had a different life. But I valued my lifestyle and thought that they were the ones missing out on the good life.

My father is Rabbi Pinchus Feldman, Dean and Spiritual Leader of the Yeshiva Centre. My mother is Rebbetzin Pnina Feldman, the daughter of Rabbi Chaim Gutnick, who came to Australia from America about 50 years ago. The Lubavitcher Rebbe sent my grandparents and parents here, even though religious life in Australia was minimal, in order that they spread the light of *Yiddishkeit*, spread the light of *Torah*. That was the purpose of their coming to Sydney. The fact that most of the family today are Rabbis shows my grandparents' strength of character — that here in Australia they were able to achieve this influence with their family and so many others in Jewish life.

My siblings are all involved in the task of spreading *Yiddishkeit*. My sister Fruma is married to Rabbi Nochum Schapiro, Rabbi and Director of Chabad House on the North Shore; my sister Nechama is married to Rabbi Levi Shemtov and currently lives in Washington, working in Jewish outreach; my brother Motti is Rabbi of the Yeshiva campus in Dover Heights and is involved in Jewish education and outreach; my sister Leah is married to Rabbi Yanky Berger, Rabbi and Director of Chabad of Double Bay; my other brothers and sister are students and are also following the same lifestyle.

We believe that the Torah is the blueprint of creation. This is a concept that I have actually never had a problem with because, ultimately, I realised how most questions could be solved and addressed in the Torah. Naturally, everyone has a mind of their own, and questions. But since the Torah is so well based, well rooted, most of my questions and problems that arose I could solve, if not all of them.

My education involved minimal secular studies. In my primary school, at Yeshiva college here in Sydney, we learned the regular secular subjects. But when I left primary school, I also left Sydney, for the Yeshiva in Melbourne, and we learned mainly Jewish and Hebrew studies, *Talmud* and *Chassidus*. By Year Nine we were learning just Jewish studies. We were taught that learning a trade or profession should be secondary to learning Torah and not the reverse and should not be at the expense of giving one's best youthful years to learning Torah. Therefore, secular studies were minimised in comparison to study of Torah.

My life concentrated on being closer to *Hashem* through learning Torah and through doing *mitzvot*. There were some sports and other activities which we engaged in to maintain a healthy and normal lifestyle but we didn't really concentrate on them. We considered them a side activity and not the main focus of our lives.

During my youth, I didn't consider the future. We were brought up to believe that *Mosshiach* could, and most likely would, come at any moment, so we only concerned ourselves with the present. We believe that *Hashem* provides sustenance. This can be seen with my uncle (mining magnate) Joseph Gutnick for example. He had limited secular studies and nonetheless became extremely successful. We rely on *Hashem* to provide for us and we do the right thing to the best of our abilities.

When one is younger one should be completely dedicated to the learning of Torah whereas when we get a little older, the Torah wants us to go out into the world, to get married and earn a living and engage in a profession. We do not have any contact with girls until that time. On the other hand, we're still human so, according to the Torah, one should therefore find himself a wife when he's 18 years old. Nevertheless, this may not be possible for a number of reasons, but still, the earlier one marries the better. I was already 21 years old when the time had come for me to get married. That's when I so-called 'got onto the market'. When people know you are ready they call a *shadchan*, or your family calls a *shadchan*, to see if they can arrange someone appropriate for you to meet.

The *shadchan*, knowing the background of both families and knowing the boy and the girl, arranges for them to meet. The boy usually takes the girl out somewhere, like the lobby of a large hotel, where the two can talk privately without the pressures of having people over them, and decide whether they are suited to each other. I met my wife like this. It just so happens that I went out with one girl initially and decided after going out a few times that we weren't suited for each other.

With the second girl that I met, the woman I eventually married, I had that feeling almost right away. It was very important that she had the same philosophies as myself and lived the same lifestyle, but it was also important to have had the feeling of compatibility. After going out just a few times, Shaina and I decided to get married. We then wrote to the Rebbe for his blessing which he gave. We have now, thank God, a very happy marriage and five beautiful children, *ken-eina hara*, two girls and three boys.

I think that some people have a misunderstanding of what *shidduchim* are all about, a misconception. They think that people are just put together randomly but this is simply not the case. We believe the lifestyle prescribed by Torah leads to success in marriage. This is clearly what the Talmud tells us about the monthly period of separation, the *mikva* and the other laws guiding married life.

The Lubavitcher Rebbe emphasised that the priority for this generation is to bring as many Jews back to *Yiddishkeit* as possible and, indeed, all of humanity closer to God. I therefore thought that in the unlikely event of *Mashiach* being delayed, I would work as a Rabbi, a teacher of Jewish studies, or some other sort of occupation in connection with Jewish education and outreach.

I am now the director and teacher of the *smicha* program at the Rabbinical College of the Yeshiva Centre. The students at the program come to the Yeshiva to study for their ordination. While also teaching and working here, I am involved as the Director of Adult Education and as required, help my father at the Yeshiva Centre.

For the past five years I have also been the rabbi at Illawarra Synagogue. Although the synagogue is Orthodox the congregation is, however, not very religious. But based on our teachings I am very tolerant of 'secular' Jews and I certainly do not consider myself greater than them. Indeed, my wife and I feel privileged that we have had the opportunity to play a role in impressing upon them the importance and pleasantness of our religion. Thank God we have succeeded in attracting, in a very practical way, many members of the community to raise their level of Jewish observance.

The reward of working with a small congregation is when I see someone who has been influenced by myself and is advancing in their *Yiddishkeit*. This is the greatest reward I can receive. The way we define someone's achievements and development in their *Yiddishkeit* is by their effort, dedication and commitment.

I feel privileged to have been brought up and to live the way I do. We may have a lot of rules but we also have a very good life. You could describe it as a situation where the short-term may be a bit difficult however in the long-term it is for the best. This is how the restrictions should be looked at in Judaism.

I am not a prophet to be able to predict the future so I can only talk about the present. I think, on the one hand the Jewish community is heading towards greater heights and on the other hand, it's diminishing. I believe there is more Jewish involvement and activity in an organisational sense here in Sydney today than twenty years ago. Part of the reason is the influence my parents have had here in Sydney through the Yeshiva and the efforts of all of its students, rabbis and lay people, inspired and directed by the Lubavitcher Rebbe. On the other hand, there is a lot of intermarriage and assimilation.

I believe I will stay in Australia until *Mosshiach* arrives. The Rebbe sent us here and it is our mission to be here. However, if a person is not involved in spreading *Yiddishkeit*, then their place is in Israel. For, indeed, it is our belief that unless Jews stay in the Diaspora for the specific purpose of assuring the continuity and survival of the Jewish community, their place, if possible, is in Israel.

Descendant of Menasseh

Miriam Samra

Miriam is a member of the B'nai Menashe, a community of around 5,000 people from the North East Indian States of Manipur and Mizoram. The Bene Menashe have emerged from the closely interrelated Chin-Kuki-Mizo group of tribes (the Chikim) of this region. Many Chikim have come to believe that they are of Israelite origin; the B'nai Menashe have acted on the strength of this belief, adopting the Jewish religion. Miriam's father, Joseph Jacob, was one of the pioneers in this movement, so that she herself has grown up strongly committed to Judaism from her childhood. However, members of her community, including Miriam herself, have had to undergo conversion to be formally accepted as Jews.

When I arrive, Miriam and her husband Myer, an anthropologist who has been studying the B'nai Menashe, have just returned home with the shopping. Their baby daughter Suzette is happily playing beside us, and with the table now laden with sweets, we begin our conversation.

When I was born, my dad already observed *Shabbat,* so I've been brought up as a *Shabbat* keeper. We'd do all the same, like in Judaism, like not eating pork. We used to have night devotions before we went to bed. Every evening Dad would have us read Psalms and Proverbs, one verse each. He taught us that when you go to other people's houses, you should not eat meat because you don't know what kind of meat you are eating. That's how we've been brought up.

Until 1972, Dad was a Pastor in the Church of God (Zionist), when he and three of his friends realised that they had to follow

Judaism, the religion of the Bible. They worked out what they should do by reading the Bible. Now there are 5,000 Jews in the area, but I can count only 16 or something Jews when I was young. Judaism spread very fast. People liked the idea, most of the people who followed my daddy when he was a Pastor, listening to his teaching. And not only my daddy, all four founders' families were good speakers.

At first we practised as Jews without any contact with the outside Jewish world, until V L Benjamin and T Daniel visited Bombay in 1975, where they met members of the Jewish community, and helped teach them to read Hebrew and to pray with the *Siddur*, and they persuaded the Director of ORT to accept some of our youngsters to train there.

Our people were now practising Jews, and from then onwards it was difficult for us in school. We become people's targets, because they didn't like the idea of Judaism and the idea of *Shabbat* keeping. So they always wanted us to convert our parents, thinking, 'If we convert the children first, so the parents will automatically follow.'

Our school was an Assembly of God school, and after that they started World Vision; support from abroad. They gave a letter to my daddy, 'Since your daughter is a scholarship student, she must attend Sunday School.' My dad said, 'She will not observe Sunday,' and they said, 'We'll give her place to someone else.' In the end, my sister didn't get the support and they gave it to somebody else. So we left the school and we went to another Christian school. I was already in Class Eight, and I felt very embarrassed because every Friday evening they had Good News Club, and I used to be late for *Shabbat*. We left one school, and already there were problems in another. And I felt very proud of my Jewishness.

At school, we had a Student Union election, and they voted me in as Secretary for the whole school. An Evangelist came and he always preached Jesus Christ, and about how no man can enter heaven except through Jesus, and the Jews killed Jesus. And all eyes were on me. Then they said, 'Whoever is born again, sit down,' and I was the only one left standing. I was the only target, because all my fellow students were Christian. They always asked 'Are you born again?' and I said, 'No, my daddy said Jesus is not God, just a human being like you and me.' So I really got upset, and I said I wanted to leave the school.

I had high marks compared to my friends and I came top of the class, but the Principal called all the teachers and said, 'Some of the subjects she must fail, otherwise it will embarrass us if a non-Christian student gets the top mark.' This was not known to me, but one of my teachers, who was an Evangelist, was very concerned about me and said, 'I am sorry. You did very well, but I have to give you a low mark.' And my mood went down and I wanted to cry. He said 'Miriam, this is not the only thing you are going to fight for.' So my daddy put me in the same school as my brother. My brother had the same problems, and my daddy got angry. He sent him to another school, and he got first place.

My Daddy says, 'Wherever you see a Jew you will see suffering. Even King David, the day God anointed him, began to suffer. So you being a Jew, you have to suffer until you reach the Promised Land, where Jews enjoy their life.'

When I finished school, I enrolled in college, and I ran a Jewish school in the community, next to the synagogue. It was called Bet Shalom JB School. I ran the school and taught, and I hired three other teachers. I started with no aid, I paid for it, like that, no support. So I didn't support my family and in 1986 I had to leave the school because it was not successful. So I started my Bachelor's degree study, and luckily I was appointed as teacher in a Presbyterian school. Still, on Sunday I taught all the Jewish children *aleph bet,* and on *Shabbat* I taught them prayers.

In 1988, they said rabbis would be coming, and they would do conversions in Bombay. And that those who did the conversion would go to Israel, and I was very happy. On 12th April I was supposed to appear in my Bachelor's finals to get my degree, but I would miss the opportunity to convert. And I wanted to finish my degree, and I was so worried about what to do. My passport already arrived. My Dad said, 'Give up the worldly things and God will be with you,' and, 'Always religion is far better than Bachelor's degree. Do the conversion and go to Israel, that is our life. I will be very happy the day you touch the ground in Jerusalem.' I wanted to make my dad happy, but to get my education was my life career. And I was torn between them. The hardest decision of my life. My daddy said 'You will be very happy later on. You have to look forward to when the happiness will come.'

We got to Bombay eventually, and the Rabbis came. The conversion was to be in Bombay, and then we would go to Israel. Rabbi Newman spent one *Shabbat* with the girls and one with the boys, and he was very angry and said no more conversions. I was very upset and I said, 'Rabbi, we are not wealthy. We have come here and it has taken three days and nights by train. We have come here, we are happy, we have high hopes.' And he said no because he saw the observance of *Shabbat* with the boys was not the same as Judaism; smoking and taking the train. And he said he doesn't want to be responsible for that.

So I was very upset and I started to cry. I felt very angry and Rabbi called me and said, 'Don't cry,' and I felt more and more like crying. Then he said, 'Okay, we will give you conversion, don't cry any more.' I was so happy, like a small child. That was my first happiness. This happiness, I never got the same again. The conversion was great. I am very happy today because I am a Jew. They gave me a conversion paper, and when I came home my daddy said, 'This is so important, we respect it as holy. We will not touch it with the head uncovered.'

MYER: Miriam was so moved when she underwent the conversion in Bombay that she wrote a song to express her joy. It's a song in praise of her father and mother, for having brought her up in Judaism, guiding her with spiritual values rather than simply to seek riches or pleasure. It became a popular song among members of the community in Manipur. Miriam wrote the song in Thadou, her first language, and it was translated into Hebrew for our wedding in Israel.

MIRIAM: I didn't go to Israel after the conversion, because I didn't get a visa. I went back to Manipur. I went to teach in the Seventh Day Adventist school. I still hoped to go to Israel, and then at last I lost my hope. We had no money, we were a poor family. My dad wanted us to go to a good school, so it was very expensive. Every year he had to spend thousands and thousands of rupees for our tuition fees and books. *Be'ezrat Hashem*, up to the youngest one we passed the matriculation. So I said, 'Dad, I don't think I can go,' and Dad said 'Take a loan. If you do not go, who will go amongst us?' Dad was in his bed, he was very, very sick at that time and he said, 'Don't worry, God gives you a chance for five minutes. You will know the time.' He said 'As soon as you step down from the aeroplane and touch the ground of Jerusalem I will be all right.' And I said 'Okay Daddy, I will go.'

That made my mind up that I should go, and I got to Israel in 1993. Israel was one hundred per cent different from what I expected. Before I thought, holy place, everyone would be good, holy. No more war, fighting, killing; people would always take the Word of God and be happy. It was not as I expected, but maybe I expected too much. Real thing, it's material world, like everywhere else. I was disappointed, but still I am happy because I fulfilled my parents' aim, and they were happy. Also, I used to read from the Bible, and now I saw Israel with my own eyes, and I thank God for that.

People treated me terribly. Sorry to say it, they are loving people, but they treat us differently, not like Jews. And that hurt because I am a Jew, proud. I thought I was going to my people, and then they said I had to do *giyur* again in Israel. I asked myself, 'Why do I stay here?' I said to Rabbi Avichail to send me back. I had been *giyur*, I didn't need a second *giyur*. Eventually I got *giyur* in '94. I was happy, but not as happy as I was in *giyur* in India.

MYER: Rabbi Avichail is the founder and Director of Amishav, an organisation dedicated to finding descendants of the Lost Tribes and helping them to return to Judaism. Rabbi Avichail was responsible for helping Miriam and other members of her group to settle in Israel. Miriam was one of a group of around 40 young Bene Menashe who'd arrived in Israel in 1993.

MIRIAM: I stayed in Israel, and that's where I met Myer. One girl told me about Myer, she said he would be coming. I don't know him, but Dad used to say a Jewish man from Australia, he came to visit us in Manipur. He is the first Jew who came to my place. In

Israel, one day he came to my class. All my friends said, 'Hey, Samra,' and I said, 'Who is he?' I knew his name but I didn't know him. We met when unfortunately one of the young girls in my group died, and I had to help the youngsters overcome their grief. Myer came to talk to me, he helped me take care of the problem, and that's how we met. That's my story.

We moved to Australia after the wedding. Here, I look after our daughter and I go around to *shiurim*, for learning. I want to go for my role in teaching again, but you need to learn more. If I want to teach Hebrew I need to learn more, and also for teaching in English, I need to learn more.

I like the Jewish community here. They are lovely and welcoming people compared to Israel. Israel I like spiritually, but not physically. You are in the land of your forefathers and you're treated like a stranger, whereas in Australia you feel you belong. But the respect and love and longing for Israel will always be in my heart.

Universal Beliefs

Juanita Stein

The daughter of artists, Juanita was sent to an Orthodox Jewish girls school and now regards herself as universal in her belief. Leading me to the back of her sparsely and oddly furnished flat, as befitting a 20-year-old musician, Juanita shows me the recently acquired puppy. We then settle into chairs in the sunroom.

I don't really understand the whole concept of an Orthodox girls high school because most of the religious girls, all the ones I knew, left school in year ten. They've become Jewish teachers, and the rest, like myself, are not religious at all. It's not where my heart is. There is a part of me that's definitely Jewish; you can't deny that. I feel a lot for Judaism but I prefer not to lead that lifestyle because it's inconvenient for what I want to do in life.

I used to have this argument on choice with a very Orthodox girl in my school all the time. This girl didn't know any better because since she was born she was brought up to believe a certain way. She'd say, 'But I choose to do this' and I'd say, 'You don't choose to because you don't really know any other way.'

We only had twelve girls in my senior year and most of us were not religious at all. A few of them were anti-religious. Maybe their parents sent them there because they wanted the kids to come home and teach them. But it doesn't work. You can't lead one lifestyle at home and another in an ultra-Orthodox school.

My parents are very understanding. It didn't really make a

difference to them if I came home and prayed for four hours or didn't at all. But I guess I don't know when the festivals are, I really don't know anything and I think they get a bit upset about it, like what did we send you to Yeshiva for 12 years for if you don't know anything.

My parents were always cool parents. There were never any outstanding issues that built a barrier between us. My parents would not freak for example if I tried my first cigarette because they've been there and done that. But for a lot of parents who grew up pretty conservatively and married at 18, there's a big generation gap.

My mum was an actress and she did a lot of TV work. She met my dad who was musician and they really wanted to break into the artistic scene and they thought Sydney was a better place so they moved from their wealthy family in Melbourne and they came to live here. My dad has been playing ever since. Recently he got a deal with the Blind Boys of Alabama, a really big blues group in America — five blind guys and they're all like eighty. They performed at the Academy Awards.

My dad's mum was Czech and she went through the war with her parents. My dad's dad is real hard yakka Aussie, the full-on type. He was a really renowned boxer in his day and worked on the farm and stuff like that. My dad left home when he was 14 and got a trade and found his own life. He was very independent. My mum's dad is Polish and her mum is Australian, so I've got a bit of Australian on both sides, but basically European is where my Jewishness comes from.

Neither of my parents were from Orthodox homes. My dad had elements of Judaism kept because of his mother — because of what she went through and what her parents went through she wanted to keep the elements of Judaism strong. As for my mum's parents, they both had very hard lives so it wasn't the most important factor. I think probably if they had a good family life, wealthy, had a nice garden and house then it would have been more important to them. I could be wrong, that's just my opinion. But apparently my great-great-grandparents were very very religious.

My dad is heavily influenced by every religion. He's not solely Jewish, he's interested in Buddhism, Confucianism, Hinduism Catholicism, very interested in Jesus, so I've got incredible background knowledge from that, learning from every religion.

If you said to me what is Judaism that would be too difficult to answer. It's very undefinable. I just believe in so many different things. It's such a clichéd answer and you've probably heard it a million times before from peers, but I'm extremely spiritual much more than I am religious.

Judaism can't be the whole truth because it doesn't free people. I see a lot of these religious Orthodox people and I respect them a lot for what they do but they're not free, they still have to work, they still have to pay for what they want, they still have to bring up about 10 children. There's a lot of stuff they have to do. No religion frees people. If all you're working for is the next life, you miss out on this one.

I would love to bring my kids up believing in everything. I'd probably send them to a non-religious school but I'd teach them that they are Jewish and that there are fundamental beliefs about Judaism they should learn about. But I would not force them to believe anything. I'd show them it isn't the only religion but this is what you are and you can't deny it.

I'd also like to marry someone Jewish — for comfort reasons. It would be comfortable for me to live with someone Jewish because there's a lot they would understand that somebody who wasn't wouldn't. There's just something undefinable. But I'd hate to discriminate against anyone and I was brought up with the belief that if you fall in love with someone who is not Jewish, as long as you love them and are truly happy, then go for it, that's all that matters. I'd never go out with someone Jewish just for the sake of them being Jewish. My current boyfriend, if he wasn't Jewish, I'd still be going out with him. But him being Jewish added to the appeal.

I feel most Jewish around the family — occasionally we have Friday night dinner. I'm not very Zionistic, not very religious, not very anything. But I'll turn on the news and see five kids killed, my age, in Israel, and I'd feel extremely Jewish all of a sudden.

I relate to the Holocaust very much because I have family who went through it and even if I didn't I have friends whose family went through it. You can't even put it into words; tragic is an under-statement. The thing that separates the Holocaust from other tragedies is that there's an element of denial in it. There's a lot of people who

161

claim it didn't happen and a lot of people who claim it's a whole lot of propaganda, that it wasn't as bad as they make out. It frustrates the hell out me because I relate to it so much.

I've heard a lot of responses to discussions we'd have at school or with my family about the Holocaust; about why the Jewish people didn't fight back. Throughout history, they haven't been known to be a physically strong race. Why couldn't a whole lot of Jewish extremists get a whole lot of machine guns and rip the Nazis' heads apart? A lot of religions and races have been persecuted throughout time but it's like Jewish people have this amazing spiritual force that I haven't really seen in any other religion. That's what they fight with — their spirit. Spirit in the long run is much stronger then physicality and you can punch someone as long as you want but if they believe it they will always be stronger then you.

I don't believe in a religion and I don't believe religion is the answer. I believe in a superior being and that we are not the only living beings in the universe and I believe in God, very much so, very strongly. And I believe that everything happens for a reason and I believe in extreme happiness and helping as many people as I can throughout my life. If I can basically just be happy and make other people happy that would be amazing. It would be such a good life rather than having all these expectations through one religion. That's not the way to go.

I want to do music. That's what gives me the most happiness and completeness. If I can make people happy through music, that would be fantastic, to relieve people of what they're feeling or give them some kind of answers to their problems. My songs are quite ambiguous but they're all pretty poetic and about life, God, love, finding happiness. A lot of them are about silly things, anything that's on my mind.

I have this saying which I'd love to go through life thinking, 'Live by intuition and inspiration and let your whole life be a revelation.' It sums up everything that I'd love to do in life, everything everyone should be doing. Through the whole religious argument, just think for yourself and do whatever makes you happy.

Reform Teachings

Paul Benjamin

Paul's mother's side is Anglican, tracing back to convict days; his father's to pre-war Germany. He is the head of Jewish studies at a primary school. We sit down to a Thai meal in the apartment Paul is minding for several months. We settle on the lounge before a table strewn with copies of the Jerusalem Report magazine and Paul, in his late 20s, begins his story.

My father arrived in Australia in 1939. He and my grandparents were the lucky ones — some of the few German Jews who had been able to obtain entry visas to Australia. They left Berlin on November 8, 1938, not realising that the notorious Kristallnacht would take place that night.

They came to Australia at a time when Germans of any type were considered suspicious. Australians seemed to be unable to understand the difference between German spies and German Jews, and they had to report to the police every week. Not surprisingly, they were quick to shed the outward signs of their ethnicity. It followed logically that Judaism was something to be practised and celebrated privately.

My mother was born in Australia. Her parents were nominally Christian. She grew up in the country, but moved to Sydney as a young adult. It must have been a big adjustment, but I think it was one that she relished. She met my father at a party, and they started to see each other. For her, it was like entering a different world. My father mixed in a very small, close circle of people he had grown up with, all of them Jewish. I know that it was a huge change for my mother, the lifestyle, the way of thinking, everything was very different for her.

I think both sets of in-laws were very happy about my parents getting married. Of course, the issue of religion came up. My mother saw how important it was for my father and offered to convert to Judaism. My grandparents had always had respect for religion. So, for them, it was not a difficult decision that their daughter had chosen to do this. She said that it made my father very happy when she offered to do that because he felt that he wouldn't be able to ask her. I don't know what would have happened if she had chosen not to but I have a sense they probably would have married anyhow.

Today, it is the Jewish festivals that tend to bring our family together. This, combined with the geographical distance, meant that I saw less of my mother's side of the family. I guess this led me to see my identity as being mainly made up of my Jewish background. Yet, on a recent trip to visit my grandfather in the town of Moruya, I really felt in a way that I rediscovered my own heritage there. I realised when I went to the small town where he grew up and drove around, that I actually had a heritage in Australia going back five or six generations. I visited the grave of my great-grandfather and it very much changed the way in which I perceived myself. Up until that time I'd perceived myself as a child of German-Jewish refugees with an Australian link. Now I see it much more in equal terms. We discovered that the first immigrant of our family to come out was actually a convict, which had been a family secret for some time.

My father's Jewish upbringing was fairly secular in that my grandparents were Reform Jews in the classical sense. They very much identified as Germans. My grandfather had fought for the Germans in the First World War and he'd been captured and sent to Siberia for some time and had won a very high medal. They both considered themselves to be very German. German first and Jewish second.

My own upbringing was strong from a cultural point of view but not particularly observant from a religious point of view. I remember having gone to a Jewish school since kindergarten. I was always aware of being Jewish and it was always celebrated in our home around the festivals and we had *Shabbat* every week. Yet, the actual observance of

Jewish laws was fairly lax. Largely, it was mother who made the home Jewish. I don't know whether that was simply because at those times the mother tended to be the one to shape much of the family life, or because of her conversion, or both. I tend to think it's probably both.

I remember coming home from school in second grade with the custom of dipping apples in honey for the Jewish festival of *Rosh Hashana*. My grandparents looked at me in an extremely puzzled way, they'd never heard of it before and they eventually just wrote it off as 'some Polish custom'. In the same way, when my parents chose to send me to a Jewish school in the first place, when I was six, my grandparents and their friends were all sitting around in a coffee shop. They talked about it and said, 'What do they want him to be, a rabbi, or something like that?'

I joined the youth movement *Netzer* when I was 13 and from the very first minute I was hooked and over many years became more and more involved, went to leadership positions and eventually ended up leading the movement on a national level, and from there it was a logical and natural step to become involved in Jewish education.

Before doing this, however, I spent a year in an advertising agency. It's a job that I thought I always would have wanted to have. I did it for a year and then felt something was missing and realised the job I also kept, the Sunday teaching at Temple, was what had really given me meaning throughout the year and that coincided with an offer of a scholarship and those feelings and that opportunity just came together and there was no turning back.

I went overseas to study for two years at the University of Judaism in Los Angeles, doing a Master of Arts in Education and a Bachelor in Literature in Hebrew Letters which is Rabbinic texts. After that I studied for an additional year in Jerusalem doing a program which brings in Jewish educators from around the world for a year of intensive study.

I now work as director of Jewish Studies at The Emanuel school. It's a progressive Jewish day school with about 550 students from the ages of five to eighteen. It's a pretty consuming job because it involves not just the academic side of Jewish life but also of the experiential side, which means all the Jewish festivals, Jewish celebrations, commemorations. We take quite a unique approach to teaching Judaism — on the one hand, it is very important for us that our students have a strong base of Jewish knowledge and skills. On the other hand, we realise that only each individual student will ultimately decide the role that Judaism will play in their adult lives. We try and give them the tools they need to make Judaism meaningful.

For my parents, this was something they've always been fairly proud of. I'm sure in some ways it would have been easier for them if I had chosen a more traditional career. But I'm sure they could also see not only was this what I enjoyed but it was what I had good aptitude for. They've always been enormously supportive.

My parents, when I was younger, were advised that I should undergo a symbolic conversion through Orthodoxy. They decided not to, more through inaction then anything else. I'm glad they didn't do it. I'm proud of my heritage as a progressive Jew and as a progressive Jewish leader. I've never felt inadequate as a Jew and I think there are some injustices in our Jewish world which deserve to be fought against and not acquiesced to.

My mum's conversion hasn't had an impact on me but the potential is always there. When I was 16, I went out with a girl who didn't identify with any religion at the time and it turns out, through her grandmother, that her mother would be considered to be Jewish. So I found myself in the rather ironic situation that here she was a totally non-identifying Jew who would be considered by Jewish law to be Jewish whereas by some people's interpretations, because my mother converted through Reform, I would be considered a non-Jew, despite all my years of involvement and how central Judaism was in my life.

I don't believe that all the years of communal bickering between Orthodox and Reform has ever produced anything positive, has ever brought one Jew back from the steps of assimilation, has ever done anything positive for the overall Jewish community. I think the situation needs to resolve itself with people moving away from movements and more to a broader understanding of what it is to be Jewish.

I think there are a lot of people who identify as Orthodox Jews but who don't meet the standards of Orthodox Judaism. It's not necessarily a criticism, there are also many Conservative and Reform Jews who the same thing could be said about, but I don't think the modern Orthodox Jewry today, where people identify with the movement but fail to live up to the basic ideals of it, I don't think that's a sustainable situation.

My feeling is that there will be a number of Jews in the Orthodox community for whom the contradiction simply becomes too great and who eventually will be forced either to change the nature of the community or move to another community. At the same time, I see a growing number of Jews who are prepared to take those leaps of faith and to embrace them and to continue on from there.

There are certainly contradictions between my role as teacher and my personal life and I'm still working out how to reconcile that. I would imagine that the only real way to do so is simply to become more of a traditional Jew, but my love of Judaism has always been from a spiritual, cultural point of view; from a point of view of a force that binds people together and really, that's the ultimate motivation for me to be able to give that gift to other people.

The favourite thing I find about being Jewish is doing the work that I do, working with children and especially with adolescents. I think it's an enormously formative time and in many ways it's a real privilege to be able to be given the responsibility of working with kids in this age to help them form an identity. For the same reason, it can also be very difficult and sometimes quite upsetting to see the failures. But the successes are very sweet.

For many years I wondered what I would do with my life, what profession I should do and it was often a cause of great concern to me. But the moment I made the decision, it all seemed so enormously clear and I couldn't see why I had taken so long to reach it.

Converting through Orthodoxy

Vaughan (Gamliel) Cobbin

Vaughan's appearance had changed since our previous meeting a couple of years earlier. Still wearing the kippa as he had done previously, he now also sports a lengthy beard and payes, or side curls, worn by some religious Jews. It's a long road from his suburban, non-Jewish background to conversion and the yeshivot of Jerusalem. He describes the journey to me on a wet evening, having just cycled to my home.

One of the most important things for this interview, I suppose, would be that both my parents are not Jewish and there aren't, to my knowledge, any Jewish people in my family. On my mother's side, there's a very strong Anglo representation. According to my mum's research, she's big into doing this right now, everyone was upper-middle class, quite well off. History has it that I'm related to a certain John of Gaunt, but I don't know who that is. My father's father was born in Australia — and that's where the trail stops — and his mother came from Scotland.

Both my parents were university people. My father was Associate Professor in pharmacology at Sydney University. My mum did a PhD in pharmacology as well, but you couldn't have husband and wife in the same faculty so she went ahead and got a degree in psychology at Macquarie University and now works at the University of Technology at my old faculty, the chemistry faculty. I've got a Bachelors degree in chemistry.

I was born in Sydney, in 1967, the only child of my mother, fourth son of my father (second marriage), three half siblings from my father's first marriage, brother and sister and another brother. I didn't grow up with them but used to see them on the weekends. I grew up in the North Shore, a very quiet place, everyone has a large block, a lot of space, there's a creek running through the yard, out of the way from everywhere, extremely quiet. I would say a difficult place for an only child to grow up, very lonesome.

You could say my family was Orthodox — orthodox atheists. I'm not exactly sure if it was orthodox atheist or orthodox agnostic but there was zero religion in my house. The only religion I remember came from my grandmother. We celebrated Christmas and Easter as family holidays. When I was young there was a Christmas tree but there was no holy spirit. We never were taken to church. I think I went to a chapel service for someone that died once and maybe one wedding. So I had no spiritual experiences growing up.

When I was young at school you had to attend scripture classes and I'd come home asking all these questions about Jesus. My mum wasn't really too keen on this God Squad stuff. She said if I'm going to have to learn this, if there's no choice, no non-scripture, then she'll put me into Jewish scripture, of all things. She felt that if you're going to learn anything you might as well learn from the Old Testament because that's got some decent stories. My mum is not a conventional woman. I remember learning the Hebrew letters, we learnt about Daniel and the thorn and Moses splitting the Red Sea. By the time I got into primary school there was non-scripture so by that time I was in a religion-free environment again.

My mum always had Jewish friends. Growing up on the North Shore, it's difficult not to encounter Jews. I had plenty of Jewish friends at school so I knew about the *Shabbos* and *mitzvots*, the concepts anyway. I had a friend whose father died in high school and he explained to me about *shiva*. And that was when I started getting a better taste of what Judaism was about.

Having very good friends who were Jews, there was always something significant for me about the more religious lifestyle. The big thing that got my attention was *Shabbat*, on Friday night doing *kiddush*, going to the synagogue and just going to people's places for *Pesach seder* and *Rosh Hashana*. I became definitely more interested, had a lot of Jewish friends and we had a good rapport and I became drawn towards the religious side of it. At that time I was also noticing the things that were missing from my family environment — that there's got to be something about the way these people live, there was a big family connection in their lives.

At the same time I couldn't get behind the whole Christian concept. There was a leap of faith as far as I was concerned which I couldn't make and I had thought about conversion for a long time. I asked myself why would you consider doing it? Why can't you just stay the way you are? Then, I think when I was about 19 or 20, I remember there was a point of accepting there was a creator and what did that mean to me. Studying science and engineering helped me along with my belief. I learnt of the scientific explanation of the creation of the world and the holes in that theory and it did not satisfy my thirst for knowledge, to know who we are and where are we are from. And the missing link, where is it? And the fact that there is another, alternative, history to the world.

So I started questioning people. What did conversion to Judaism mean? Can one really be a part of what's going on? Getting to know religious people. I worked for a kosher caterer for a long time and learnt a lot there. I attended synagogue services, *chagim*, Friday night dinners, learning more about it. I found, in general, the Jewish community in Sydney to be very welcoming, some people may have been a tiny bit prejudiced, like 'You're not part of things, you don't belong.' They were wary but open.

I would have been 22 or 23 when I finally decided to convert. I planned to make the move when I finished university. But there came a point when I thought, 'If you really believe in this why are you waiting, start now, let the powers that be know that you are interested.' I always saw it as a step for life, you don't just do it and in five years' time say, 'Yes, I was into it, I really was once into it.' I didn't want to be one of those people.

In my research, I investigated all the various types of Judaism and the concepts of Reform and Conservative Judaism didn't appeal to me for the same reasons that I wasn't interested in Christianity, or Islam for that matter. I believe what we have in the Torah is the truth.

Nobody really knows what's written in there but from what we do know, there is the truth. The written and oral Torah, they complement, they are one and the same thing, they're connected, and through study of this, we learn the world's secrets.

I also researched the whole Sephardi thing so I went to see what was happening at the Sephardi synagogue on a Friday night. And here I found that extra little, that certain aspect of public worship that was missing from the other synagogues and that was it for me, that was the missing little key, this really is community-based, it's not just me, it's not just my family, it's part of being a Jew. It was all very emotional in those days and all I knew was that it fitted. I was especially impressed with the rabbi and his knowledge, he is definitely one of the more learned rabbis, he grew up in Israel and attended various *yeshivot* and was of Sephardi background.

I told him my name, where I was from, I said 'I came to see you to introduce myself to you, I come from a non-religious, no particular, Christian background. I realise you're on the *Beth Din* and I'm very interested. I realise that you have to push me away, so tell me how many times I've got to come back and I will. I don't mind.' He questioned me a bit about my family background, that kind of stuff and I basically started going to that synagogue, whenever I could. From that time on I was definitely quasi-observant, I was like a non-religious Orthodox Jew. I hadn't entered the program yet, I decided before you waste anybody else's time, spend a year doing it and see if you can do it, can you deal with the physical aspects, kosher food, not eating milk and meat together, ignoring Friday night as an night of entertainment and going out, going to regular prayer? So I passed my own personal test and said, are you going to do the business or what? Then I started meeting, going to various interviews at the *Beth Din*, which were interesting. Rabbi Sevi did try to discourage me, made things sound much less attractive than they were, brought up various problems like you'll get bored, it's not going to be interesting for you, you'll lose the charge, you'll want to move on, and I was ready and prepared for that.

The whole process would have taken about five or six years but the conversion process itself was rather swift, about a year. But I did have references, people knew I had been attending synagogue, they knew I was serious. Looking back on it I was serious, a bit naive, didn't know the full picture. But I knew that I happened to pick what is the correct path.

The conversion was a milestone, definitely was a big milestone, a huge sense of relief, a goal. I reached it and now it's for real, you passed the test. Like in driving you now have the responsibility not to hurt people by reckless driving, you now know the rules and you have to drive safely within the rules. My first *call-up* was on *Shabbat mincha*, it would have been my bar mitzvah, my Jewish birthday. The final process was, usually you have a *bris mila*, but I was circumcised shortly after birth so a symbolic drawing of blood from the site, just a drop or two, then you go into the *mikva* and say the *brachot* and are asked the final questions: Do you realise that this is what you're in for? Do you realise that you could be asked to lay down your life for example like the people who had to in the Second World War? Do you realise there may be inquisitions and not renouncing your faith? Do you realise you're taking on the *mitzvot*? Do you understand the tenets of Judaism? Are you willing to believe only in *Hashem*? And I realised that I was prepared for that.

I definitely lived an Orthodox lifestyle. Definitely wasn't going out driving on *Shabbat*. When I first finished school, I'd go down to the pub on Friday nights, have a pizza and hamburger, be a larrikin, go up the beach on Saturday, go see bands, drink some beer, have a barbie, and girls, that's something we were all interested in.

One *Shabbat* I went to dinner and I was going to walk from there to this end-of-year function for my university courses. So afterwards, I walked over there, had a prepaid ticket and my name was on the door. I didn't carry anything with me because it was *Shabbat*. I went there and it wasn't such a big event. I realised that I didn't need that, I realised the *Shabbat* was more important.

I decided to go to Israel to improve my Jewish knowledge for a year. I was 25, not so old, and had various work-experience in my field. I realised that once I settled down I wouldn't have the opportunity to see what the *yeshiva* is, what learning is and how other Jews live. To see what it's like living in a more vibrant Jewish community. I was definitely going for a year only and not planning to live there.

I started off on a kibbutz and didn't like it much. It was religious but on a slightly lower level than I wanted. When *Pesach* came along and I spent it with my *Rav* at his family's place, that was it for me, I got into a *yeshiva* and was living at the *yeshiva*. It was an open *yeshiva* and not very overbearing. They have non-religious people there and the idea is that if you want to come and study you're welcome, and that was a brilliant environment, not highly regimented. I started with the introductory *gamera shiur*, Jewish philosophy, seminars on Judaism.

The first year, I was just learning, pulling in more information, committing myself to learning on a regular basis. And when the year finished, I wanted to go back home, finish my last subject at uni, sort things out, and come back again. I got stuck here for a while and then got a round-the-world ticket to go and see if *yeshiva* is for me. If it was, to come back to Sydney and pack up and go. And if it wasn't for me, to come back and settle down in Sydney.

But it was for me. I got introduced to a girl, a very nice girl, never actually married her but I was engaged to her at one stage. Maybe that's one of the things I feel was a mistake, not going for it 100 per cent. But there were various factors involved, it was cultural, and there were family issues involved as well. I got engaged and came back to announce the news and went to my university graduation. My mum then said she wanted to meet the girl, to pay for her to come out to visit my relatives, just to see the city where I came from so she knows who I am, my background, which in itself was a very good idea. My mum developed a great relationship with the girl, they were in communication for a long time, my mum diagnosed one of her health difficulties over the phone. Her parents were divorced and because she was under 18 at the time she wasn't allowed to leave Israel without a letter of release from both parents and her mother was saying no. And my mum said she could organise for her to stay with an Orthodox family, we just want to meet her. That became a problem and I was stuck and we had to wait till her 18th birthday but I just had to get to Israel; I really wanted to get back. I saved up my money and I went. Things then became a bit difficult and then it was kind of off and then some people were working for it to be on again, so it came quite close but it didn't quite match. It changes one's life. She got married, had a child, and lives in England.

I moved to Jerusalem and had a hard time finding an apartment to live in. I definitely experienced difficult times that first year, financially tough times. I was a little bit outside the general regulations because I hadn't made *aliyah* so there were jobs I couldn't do, most jobs. I supported myself doing jobs you're not meant to do like working as a cleaner, cash in hand. I made a living cleaning stairwells, a little bit of carpentry, painting, general handyman work. And I was also studying.

I ended up in a place with a friend I'd known for a few years. I was staying at his place in the interim and he said you can stay here if you want, and I wanted to contribute rent and he said, 'It's all taken care of, you don't have to pay rent,' a very open guy, very generous, just had a baby, may it be the will of *Hashem* that it's a healthy baby and the first of many.

I came back to Australia this time as I hadn't seen my mum for almost two and a half years, and my great-aunt is over a hundred. I'm here to catch up with family and friends, and organise my finances so I didn't have to worry about income tax, so it's all done automatically, store my things, get my books sent over and go back to Israel. I'll stay in Israel but I'm not sure if I'll be a citizen, but I will definitely be a permanent resident.

I let my brothers and sisters break the news of my conversion to my dad. I told him I couldn't come to him because it was *Shabbat* and it was a Jewish thing and that's what I'm doing now, so he knew something, and they were coming up to tell him the rest. He was fine. It actually turned out that my dad was very interested in the concept. His dad had almost converted to Judaism when he was a younger man, about my age. That's what my brother told me.

My mum didn't really react as well. She's not into religion at all, doesn't like the concept. Culturally, she can deal with things but not otherwise. As one of my friends pointed out the other day, my mum embracing the idea of me getting married to a religious girl from Israel wasn't a problem. So she's not against the concept, but I guess there's an ideology clash. But she does want me to be happy and one of the goals of this trip is to get closer to her.

My secular friends I relate to reasonably well. It's a difficult point when you see something and you're sure it's the right way, you do have the urge to go to people and say how can you not see, but you can't force people with that kind of approach. Some of my friends, I think, when they see me they get a 'There must be something to it' feeling, it may inspire someone to do a *mitzvah* here and there. I kind of let them know if they ever want to talk to anyone about religion, if they want to learn with someone, they can ask a question and I'll do whatever I can to the best of my abilities. But we have demarcation lines.

Young Jews, I think, are going away from Judaism because there's nothing really there for them, there's no community. That's actually one of the most bothersome things in the world Jewry. Everyone, secular, religious, belongs to quite a specialised little religious group they identify with, where they have shared ideologies. And the more private people get, living hidden away in the suburbs, the more space between you and your nearest Jewish neighbour, means there's no connection. The unifying thing is whether there's a God and tradition and Israel.

My relationship with Judaism is changing. I'm definitely getting on a more intimate emotional level. There's following the laws on one level, where you don't deviate. You get up in the morning and wash your hands in the right way, say your prayers. Everything in the right order in accordance with the strict interpretations. But you just do it and your mind isn't really on it. Then there are the kind of people that get up in the morning and their first thought is, 'What should I do today? How can I serve the Lord better?' There's a goal. I want to be a real Jew and the goal is to find the answers, to know.

I want to do what *Hashem* wants of me. How we behave towards our fellow human beings is incredibly important, how we behave in the world, how we behave as Jews. Being Jewish is being alive. You're more alive and everything can have more meaning, drinking a glass of water, a little bit of shade on a hot day. You stop taking things for granted, you notice and give thanks to where they come from.

Journey from Ethiopia

Debritu Alemeneh

Debritu is an Ethiopian Jew, a descendant of the tribe of Dan, the majority of whom were secretly airlifted to Israel in the mid 80s in what was known as Operation Solomon. She grew up in the villages of Gondar before fulfilling her dream and emigrating to Israel. There she met her husband Ian, who is Australian. Having put the kids to sleep, and aided by Ian, she recounts her story.

DEBRITU: I was born in Ethiopia, in Wyn'yee. I grew up there till I finished high school. Both my parents were born in Ethiopia and my mother died when I was young. My father is a kess, like a rabbi.

Life in Ethiopia is completely different from here and Israel. Most of the people do agriculture. I grew up in the Gondar region in a small village, maybe 100 families.

My father worked as a kess around his village, celebrating the holidays like *Sukkot, Rosh Hashana, Pesach.* Around our village there was one kess, but there were a few in Ambover, 20 minutes walking from our village. I was studying primary school in Ambover, I walked there every day. He didn't get any pay for being a kess. He just go to people and blessed. He was a farmer, wheat, corn and teff, a special Ethiopian grain. We sold these and bought things like salt, chilli, butter and clothing.

There were no cars in the village, people rode horses, donkeys and mules. There was no electricity, only kerosene lamps and wood fires.

The land was owned by non-Jewish people and Jewish people worked there. They rented, but the rent was nothing, you could pay like, 25 kilos of wheat or corn or whatever. I worked from when I was four years old. I looked after the cows and donkeys and I farmed on the land, for example, there was a bull which the boys led and after I followed and separated the weeds. There was plenty of food.

Our family was rich, we had everything. If someone has a horse that means they are rich. If they have 100 animals or more then they are rich. Cows produce milk and you can make your own butter. Once we bought a radio and to have a house with a radio was something special, and to have a tin roof, that was a luxury.

When my father was little, his father died. He tried to separate two people fighting and they shot him. His father was pretty young when he died, maybe 24 or 25.

My father had a very hard time, a very hard life. He was born in 1913 and he's still alive, in Israel. He had a godfather and he was like a Jewish monk, they lived in a separate place, no women there, only men, and they worked by themselves and they prepared food and they studied there. They studied for 10 years, like in a *yeshiva*.

My mother didn't have any education. She met my father through a *shidduch*. She was pretty young when she married, probably 13 or 14 years old. She died when she was 48 years old. I had just finished primary school.

We were 11 children from my mother and father and another five from my father and his new wife. My father remarried a woman about my age, a young woman. If you are a kess you don't marry someone if they are married before so he married a young woman. He had one boy last year and my oldest sister is in her fifties.

He was a kess and people invited him to bless when someone was born. After someone was born the woman was kept separate, if a boy, for 40 days and if a girl, for 80 days, after that they invited the kess to bless.

IAN: The woman has to live in a separate hut on the edge of the village with the baby because, according to the Torah, she's impure for that period. Then they have the *mikva* in the river followed by a party.

177

When her stepmother arrived in Israel in 1986 with her father she was nine months pregnant and gave birth two weeks later. After she had the baby they arranged in the absorption centre a special caravan for her to stay in for the 80 days.

DEBRITU: Also after a woman's period she was separated for seven days. This was generally followed by Jewish women while they lived in their villages.

IAN: Her father was very observant, very strict himself, but he didn't impose anything on the kids.

DEBRITU: My father was very open minded and he let all the kids do what they want. He didn't force us to do anything and he didn't marry us off. He married the first girl off, and after that he said he didn't want to anymore because she didn't like her marriage. She married when she was little and she always wanted to go to Israel like her sister. The woman is dominated by the man in Ethiopia so I'm very lucky.

My second oldest sister, when she was 12 years old, went to Israel. That was in 1956. And after that he said everyone if you want to study do what you want and if you want to marry you can marry. My friends my age had kids already at that time, they married when they were young, forced by their families. I could have had 10 kids by now. That's what your life is like.

I chose to do commerce, they start in Year 9. All the books are in English. And after I did my exams in Year 12. I went to teach in a village far from Ambover, for national service.

I had very bad time during the revolution. We weren't allowed to go out. They would come and take you to the prison without any trial. So at that time I stayed for one year out of school. The government didn't allow for the students to be part of the party so they decided to catch the students and take them to prison.

IAN: Mengistu came to power in the mid-70s after Haile Selassie fell about 73 or 74. It took a little while for the revolution to go through

Ethiopia and then they had what they call the Period of Red Terror in the late 70s where he tried to impose his power across the whole of the country. Because it was mainly the students who opposed the government, they were scared of people who had a reasonable education or questioned things.

Debritu has plenty of bad memories of that time. She hasn't told you everything about the revolution and people being killed.

DEBRITU: I had a bad time. At that time my mother died.

I decided to go to Israel after I finished school. I always prayed to go to Israel, all the time since I was little. Because of my sister and all the time thinking Israel is Eden, like a paradise. All the time we heard news and wanted go there. So I said after I finished my school I wanted to go and my sister sent me an invitation to study in America. My sister sent money to me, like a hundred dollars every few months. That was a lot of money, you were rich, could live for a few months on that.

IAN: After the revolution no one could leave Ethiopia, the borders were closed more or less. There was one way you could legally leave the country and that was if you were invited to study overseas after you finished high school, matriculated. Debritu and maybe 100 more got to Israel that way. They had received an invitation from a university overseas. Jews from North America and Europe organised this.

DEBRITU: It took me one year to get my exit permit to Israel. I went to Gondar six times, there was a lot of corruption. In the end my uncle, he's well known in Ethiopia, spoke to a relative who had connections in the office that granted exit permits. After I suffered one year and I stayed with my auntie in Adis Ababa, then they let me out.

When I got my visa that was the happiest time of my life. I got my visa and a week later I flew to Israel. I was nineteen.

IAN: Until the mid 1800s there weren't any ties between Ethiopian Jews and the rest of the world. Then European Jews started hearing of missionaries going to Ethiopia to convert some Jews there. So the

Alliance Israélite Universelle organisation in France sent Yosef Halevi there in 1867. When he got there not only did he find there were people practising Judaism but he was also shocked when they didn't realise he was Jewish. They didn't know there were any white Jews.

About 1904, Yakov Faitlovich, inspired by Halevi, went on his first trip to Ethiopia. He was the one who connected Ethiopian Jewry with European Jewry and created the interest in them. From that period they established a Hebrew school in Addis Ababa, in the 20s, which was closed down by the Italians when they invaded Ethiopia. These were re-established in the 50s with the help of the Jewish Agency.

Between 1904 and 1956 there were about 40 Ethiopians who went overseas, and some came back and became leaders within the Jewish community or within the government itself, and in academia. So it was an interesting situation where there were some Jewish people in high positions.

Although they weren't accepted automatically as Israeli citizens under the law of return, Yitzhak Ben Zvi, Israel's second president, was supportive. In the early 50s, after Yitzhak Ben Zvi and Yakov Faitlovic had lobbied a lot, the Jewish Agency brought out the first two groups of 20 or so to Israel from Ethiopia. Debritu's sister was in that group. It's quite amazing when you think her dad would send his daughter to Israel at the age of twelve. It was a big thing in Ethiopia, those groups went to Addis Ababa and had an audience with the Emperor Haile Selassie.

They learnt in Israel for two or three years and they went back to Ethiopia to teach. Her sister stayed on in Israel, she didn't go back.

They had a lot of difficulties. They could stay in Israel as residents but they weren't accepted as Jews. Then Ovadiah Yosef, the chief Sephardi Rabbi, in late 72, decreed they were Jews, descendants of the Tribe of Dan. And then a year or two later the Ashkenazi Chief Rabbi affirmed that. But by that time the revolution had already happened in Ethiopia and the gates were closed.

DEBRITU: When I got there, Israel was different, it was nothing like what I expected. I thought it was religious and it was completely different. I thought it would be a paradise and it wasn't a paradise. I was expecting no one to work. I was disappointed people weren't religious, not keeping *Shabbat,* but I was happy to leave Ethiopia for Israel.

It was a bit hard because of the different colour. People say 'you *kushit*', *kushit* means black. People looking at you. It was probably curiosity. We were taking a bus and people coming and looking and saying look *kushit*. It was a bit disappointing but we get used to it. There were also some good people, but not all. In Israel people like to talk, they don't keep things in their mind, they say what they think. In Ethiopia people keep more to themselves, very quiet people.

IAN: At the time she left, in 1983, that was just before the first big exodus of Jews across the border into Sudan, Operation Moses. Soon after Debritu got to Israel, people started leaving Ethiopia. But because of the collective punishment, people didn't say they were escaping because they were scared that if the police knew your relative was gone they would torture you. So her sister up and went one night.

DEBRITU: I didn't hear from her for six months, didn't know what happened to her.

Ian and I met at *Ulpan*. I arrived four months before him with my cousin. There weren't many Ethiopian students there, maybe four. We didn't think then we would be like this, married, but it continued.

IAN: In 1987 my sister got married in Australia so I invited Debritu to come out for the wedding and meet the family. We were here for six weeks and then we went back to Israel and worked and a year later we came out here to live. My sister heard I had an Ethiopian girlfriend and I sent photos and I'd been involved in Ethiopian Jewry so they got used to the idea and my family were very accepting.

DEBRITU: My family was happy because Ian was good with my family, he got on well with them. My father said he is a very good person.

IAN: Except they didn't like my gefilte fish, it was too spicy.

We've got two little kids now and we speak to them in Hebrew. They'll grow up here but no doubt we'll go back and forth and visit.

DEBRITU: I'd like to take the kids to Ethiopia one day for a visit. I miss the fresh air of Ethiopia, the natural environment.

IAN: Taking the kids to Ethiopia will be like European Jews going to Poland to learn about their background. I've got lots of info taped. When we visited Israel four years ago I taped her father going though all the *brachot*, about four hours of it. So we have stuff to show the kids. We have tapes of how they left Ethiopia through the Sudan and, interestingly, her sister and brother-in-law are in that as well. We've also got tapes of Ethiopian kids' choirs from Israel which Yoni loves to watch, and even Ben started to watch. We've started introducing them to their background: Australian, Ethiopian and Israeli.

Also my family is very traditional and every Friday night we get together for Shabbat. *We have them booked into a Jewish school and they go to the Temple pre-school.*

When we went to see Fiddler On the Roof, *Debritu could feel comfortable with it because it was traditional village Jewish life, not the same customs as in Ethiopia but it reminds you a bit of the strong, closed and vibrant community.*

DEBRITU: My village was similar to those European villages in the 18th and 19th century.

All in the Family

Tom Reed and Jackie Reed

Although siblings and only two years apart, Tom and Jackie hold very different views on life and religion. In their early thirties, both live in shared houses. We meet in the living room of the semi which Tom shares with two others, who are also friends of Jackie's.

TOM: I'm not very good on our family background. We don't have much of a family anymore, mainly due to the war.

They all came here in 1956, by boat. They had the revolution in Hungary and saw it was a good time to get out. They came out here and they didn't have anything. They started working and thirty years later they have a family, car, house.

JACKIE: Our parents both came from separate country towns. My mother's parents owned a shop and they all worked there but, of course, after the war, that was all gone, so my grandmother — she lost her husband, my grandfather, early on — had to support my mother, she had to go out and work, they didn't have very much of anything. Mum always used to say she was a latch-key kid because her mum was always working. When she came home from school, she would let herself in and look after herself.

My dad's family were not wealthy but middle class. He had a large family and they were happy, they seemed to spend a lot of time together, having big family gatherings. But they must have sensed something was happening because my grandfather told my father that whatever he does

*in life he has to get a trade because there is nothing surer then a trade.
And that's what he did, he became a cabinet-maker. Dad was very
intelligent, he wanted to be lawyer, but because of the war and
circumstances, that never happened.*

*He was originally called Rehberger. All the Jews had German names
in Hungary and after the war none of them wanted German names so
they changed them to Hungarian-sounding ones. So from Rehberger it
became Redei and then when they came to Australia it was difficult for
people to pronounce so it became Reed.*

TOM: My grandmother survived the Holocaust with the greatest
difficulty. She had the hardest job because my mum was only a little
baby, five or six years old. She was really brave, my grandmother.
They went through a lot together. There was one time my mother was
really sick, they were living on a farm in Austria, and the doctor who
was giving out the food rations said to my grandmother, 'Don't
bother giving any food rations to your daughter, she's going to die
anyway, might as well keep it for yourselves.' My grandmother, of
course, became infuriated. Thankfully, there were kids who came
from the local area who used to throw food to my mum, she used to
eat whatever they threw and eventually she got better.

Then they were at a work farm, working in manual labour, and as
the Jews got rounded up in 1944, towards the end of the war, they
went to Bergen Belsen for three months.

In the war Dad went to a work camp. He was a cabinet-maker
and he ended up making holes in the road for the tanks to fall in.
But as the Germans were retreating, the armies used all the main
roads and Dad and all the workers were using the mountain passes
to get back. They were marched, they used to shoot bullets to get
them to move on. It was so hot during the day and at night it was
freezing cold. Dad and his friends had two blankets between four of
them and each night it was somebody's turn to sleep in the middle,
and he used to tell me they used to love to sleep in the middle
because of the body warmth.

Eventually, as Dad was retreating on the mountain passes, he saw
the Germans were retreating, losing the war, it was just a matter of

time. Then they got to a *lager* somewhere, a Jewish holding camp, and they woke up in the morning and all the Germans were gone, the Russians had arrived.

JACKIE: After the war, a lot of people were going to Israel. My uncle, my dad's younger brother, tried to escape to go to Israel and they caught him. He was denounced. They had this great policy of denouncement in communist countries, where people delighted in telling the authorities about someone who'd gone against them. So he was denounced by some young girl he worked with, so he spent about three years in jail. So at that time my father couldn't leave because his brother was in jail.

But dad didn't really want to go to Israel because he felt he'd struggled enough during the war and he felt that to go to Israel would be another struggle. My grandmother at one time did want to escape to Israel with my mother but something happened. They were supposed to go with some people but they left without them. So in the end they came to the decision to come to Australia. My mother actually wanted to come here. She was about 19 and she said she wanted to get as far away from Europe as possible.

She did not know my father then, they came here individually, completely separately. My parents would have got here about the same time. That was a time when everyone was escaping.

Dad is 12 years older than my mum. He was in his thirties when he came here. He was married before my mum. He got married shortly after the war when he was only about 23 and that marriage lasted a year, if that. It was definitely a marriage of security, he lost all his family. It's interesting that my grandmother also married at the same time, also to someone who she was only married to for one year before they got divorced, and it seems that people had this insecurity and need to get married.

They would have arrived in Australia in February 1957. There was the Joint organisation, there were Jewish welfare groups, where people gathered. To actually come into the country they had to be sponsored by someone, so Jews who were already living here, who were quite wealthy, or even if they weren't, they sponsored anyone, it didn't matter who.

TOM: They struggled when they got to Australia. Grandfather cleaned toilets for a long time, grandmother worked sewing handbags because she could sew. To my father, trying to set himself up in business, he was treated harshly. He had to pay his learning money like everyone else and he worked day and night because people didn't pay, they said, 'He's only a New Australian, what's he going to do about it.' I know he struggled hard. At one stage, he had his own business with a partner and my father was working night and day and the business wasn't making any money. My mum actually threatened him, 'Look, it's not working out, you've got to leave him or me.'

I think it's one of those things that these people were very strong, they survived the war, they struggled, they had nothing but they were doers, they knew what hardship was, and they worked hard.

He opened his own furniture factory called Davis and Reid in 1967 and they bought the land with the factory and that's when he became established. In lean times, he made enough to survive and in the good times he'd take the cream off the top.

JACKIE: I think about what they went through a lot. I'm always thinking I have such a good life, such a lucky life, and you feel a certain amount of guilt that your parents didn't have that and now if you have problems of any sort they're a bit diminished by the problems they had at your age and that's something I've had to get over, that feeling of guilt and not having suffered as they have, so if I'm feeling depressed, what am I feeling depressed about, not having to worry about survival.

TOM: When I think of their experience, it's like the animal kingdom, survival of the fittest. I think the human race is now past that, we try to keep everyone alive. But in those days it was a struggle, you really worked hard to survive. I think we're the lucky generation. We just came in, we didn't have to go to war, we're well-educated, well-fed, we didn't have to struggle for our existence, we were handed it on a plate. No wonder we're doing all right in society today.

I don't think being Jewish is a problem in Australia. I think in Australia there are so many ethnically diverse groups that people can just as easily hate the Jews as they hate Muslims or Buddhists, it's not an issue in Australia, where there are so many splinter groups.

My family were fairly religious, they kept *Yom Kippur*, the main festivals. My father's father also went to synagogue, taught my dad how to read Hebrew, showed him how to follow the service. I think they were religious in those days. My father, as time goes by, still keeps the festivals. But I think he's become less and less oriented towards being kosher or wearing *tefilin*. I think he just thinks that's ridiculous.

JACKIE: In our home we kept all the major holidays. We went to a Jewish kindergarten and then we went to Sunday school after that. They didn't want us to go a Jewish high school or primary school because they thought we were very impressionable at that age and they didn't want us to be brainwashed, to become more religious than they were and make them keep kosher or something. They wanted us to know about our heritage and understand the religion but not to practise it religiously.

TOM: I loved my bar mitzvah. I remember my dad's partner Mr Davies gave me $1,000. The man was one of the greatest persons I've ever met in my life. He was Czech, had amazing war-time experiences, a very brave man, very strong man. Without him being in partnership with my dad I don't think we would ever have got where we are today. This man used to work 24 hours a day as hard as he could. So he gave me $1,000 and I remember I looked at him, I could see it in his eyes, he knew what it's like to earn $1,000. I worked in the factory for a week sweeping floors and got paid $10 and for him to give me $1,000! I thought I had become a man.

I had to study my bar mitzvah, study that stupid text, whatever it was, I couldn't understand it but I could read Hebrew, I sang it, I had a good voice at the time. My father went to extravagant lengths to put on a huge bar mitzvah. We had a band, hundreds of guests.

I find religion a bit of a joke. I find it hard that some people can be religious up to a point, something can be kosher but not overly religious. Some people can wear *payes*, *kippah* and go to synagogue every day. I just can't see that if there is a God, and I hope there is, there's obviously some supreme being out there, I think you judge people for who they are and how they perform to their fellow man and I don't think whether they're kosher or whether they didn't keep *Yom Kippur*, I don't think it makes much difference in the end. I think I'm past that. I think in the modern world, as we get more information together, religion becomes less and less likely and in the olden days you can understand how the masses were poor, they had to feed them religion, they had to have something to look forward to in the next life. As we find out more and more about the universe, religion will play a smaller role, as people interbreed. I'm hoping that peace in the world comes when everyone marries everyone, there is no this is a Catholic or a Jew, they're just people.

I think the Jews have been leaders throughout history and this one God theory, personally I think it's a good idea, it seems logical to me, I can go along with that. But I think the notion that we are the chosen people, we're better than other people, no, I don't think that's right at all. And I think that's where religions have problems. I think if there's a supreme being, whoever he is, he would treat everyone as an equal. How you treat other people and what you do to your environment, I think that's important. I can't see how losing Jewish identity is a problem. I think the tradition is nice. We'll keep the traditions, sure.

I'd probably teach my kids their heritage and background and give them a chance to embrace Judaism if they like. But I think on the whole I'd be more keen that my son or my daughter gets a general understanding on life, and I think the Jewish aspect is important but the world is a giant oyster out there and there's a lot to know.

My best friend is a Jewish boy and he married a girl who isn't Jewish and five years ago, when we were 24, 25, attitudes were a little bit different. A lot of parents, Jewish parents, a lot of people at the time thought it was a bad move. My friend's been married for six years now, they've had a baby, she's a fantastic wife, great marriage. They've got a fantastic life, I haven't got enough nice things to say about her, and she's not Jewish and therefore I think I have to reason on that basis whether I marry Jewish or not it's not going to make a great difference to my life.

JACKIE: I think it's important to know about the Jewish religion if you are Jewish, to understand your heritage, your roots, and where you come from and I think the division between religions is based on ignorance. We should study our own religions and we should study other religions. The spiritual aspect of religion is very important and everyone should have an element of spiritualism in their lives because we need that hope to carry us through our lives. But I'm not religious and I don't believe in all the stories of the Jewish religion. While I think the seeds of it are beautiful, it's similar to the seeds of other religions, they all preach be good to your fellow man, not to kill, honour your parents and elders and I think that's beautiful and I think religion is more a spiritual thing of love that you should be able to love everybody and I think religions that teach you to hate other religions are ridiculous and they engender hate instead of love and I don't think that's what religion is about.

Spirituality is constant in my life because I meditate regularly and to me that's a very spiritual experience. When I'm meditating, I feel at one with the universe. It works very well for me. Every day some part of spirituality comes into it.

I think it's very important for people to learn about their roots. In this life, we need to gather as much knowledge as possible because the whole point of life is to understand life and when you reach your final days you should have come to some understanding of what this life is and why we've lived it and its importance in history. So it's important to know as much as possible about everything.

I wouldn't say I definitely would want to marry someone Jewish but somehow life is easier when your partner understands your background and you have some type of bond. So I wouldn't exclude a Jewish partner or say my partner would definitely have to be Jewish. My parents always wanted us to marry Jewish partners since my brother and I are both over 30 now and both of us are single, I think they'd be happy for us to marry anyone at this point. Mum would be very happy.

I think because we're a minority, everyone is scared the religion might die out if everyone marries out and eventually there would be no one left. It's the importance of carrying on our heritage and tradition, which I think is an important thing. I think religion is

189

divisive, religion as it's carried out now because religions are pitted against each other.

These people who are ultra-religious, I don't think they're living true life, they're living a story; they're not being true to real life. They're trying to preserve Judaism exactly as it was and it's losing its relevance today. You should be flexible — rules don't last forever. God might have changed his mind by now. They're only seeing life from one point of view and that's not the way to experience life. To experience life you should try and understand it from as many different angles as possible and try to understand why someone else sees it differently, but to shut yourself off I think is a terrible thing and I really think the Jews have put themselves up there for the hatred that's there. They've segregated themselves, they've made themselves out to be better than everyone else; they talk of themselves as the chosen people and that's a sure way for people to hate you.

TOM: I really hope there's something out there. I'm an optimist. As a realist you'd have to say chances aren't good but I figured if I'm true to myself, love my family, respect my friends, so I think if there is any next life I'm a candidate.

There's times when I have turned to religion. I've had a few tight calls in my life. I can think of one particular time in Italy, well all I remember is there were police there and I was very grateful that nothing happened. I remember saying I'll certainly keep *Yom Kippur* that year.

It's usually in adversity and later on when you're calm, cool and collected you think differently. Jewish people have been around since day dot, so I think being Jewish is a way of life for so many people, been handed down for generations, the Ten Commandments handed down in Mount Sinai, so there's a lot of history, and because the Jewish people being persecuted against year after year, from pogroms in Russia, to the Second World War, I guess there's a certain bond there that we should stick together and fight that, but at the end of the day, I think humans are above that and one day we'll get a threat from outside — a different world — and it will be their world and our world and people will join together and will act as one.

I think I've figured it out. I've had 30 years and we only get 70 or 80 years on the earth and time, it's all about time. Everyone gets a certain amount of time and for me I don't want to be working all my life. I want to be doing what I enjoy doing and I figured if I work hard for another ten that'll be it, I can retire, play golf, lunch, go to a cafe. I really think that if I got to achieve my ideal goal I'll be living six months here and six months over in Europe, travelling around, it would be lovely to do that, have income from here and not have to worry about money.

I'm a claims manager for MMI insurance, look after workers' compensation claims, pretty unexciting nine-to-five sort of stuff. I hope I'm going to get a promotion in the next few weeks, get a company car, get a packaged position, look after a larger portfolio. Hopefully, I can get national within a year or two. I've done a real estate course — I've got six months left to do and I always figured that if I get bored with insurance I'll finish my real estate degree and become a real estate agent. Life is just cruising along at the moment. It's easy, get paid very good money, don't work too hard; have a few stresses but the rest of my energy gets spent on what I want to do to, enjoy myself.

JACKIE: I'm studying to be a naturopath. It was a number of experiences that led me to that. I was working in Japan in Tokyo, the biggest consumer society around with everything based on technology and modernism and after three years of living in such an intense society then travelling to Thailand and India, where I was living mainly in the countryside, I realised the differences and how important it was to maintain our roots with nature because, after all, we are from nature and I wanted to learn that connection with nature and I think it's of fundamental importance actually. When I finish studying, I want to open a clinic offering people education into their health and different ways of approaching it and ways to take the responsibility for their own health.

TOM: I think me and Jackie are fundamentally different. She follows what she believes and I follow my belief. I don't think we have all the

191

answers yet. I think if I had all the answers I'd know just what to do. For me the only answer is the time factor, that on any given day, I want to do what I want to do and in order to achieve that in today's world, I need to have lots of money.

JACKIE: We have such different views because in our family we were really encouraged to think for ourselves, always encouraged to speak up, never shushed and our different views were respected and we used to have vigorous family arguments but they were all in good fun and we were encouraged to develop individually, we weren't forced to conform to anything and I think we both followed our own paths.

TOM: I think in five hundred years this discussion will be dated, pointless, and religion will be a thing of the past because we'll have enough knowledge to get past that and, when we do, this will all be trivial.

Glossary

Aguna — literally 'chained'; a woman whose husband has not granted her a Jewish divorce

Aleph Bet — Hebrew alphabet

Aliyah — literally 'ascending', migrating to Israel

Ashkenazi — Jews from west, central and eastern Europe

AUJS — Australasian Union of Jewish Students

B'nai B'rith — Jewish service organisation

Bar mitzvah — coming of age of Jewish boys, age 13

Bat mitzvah — coming of age of Jewish girls, age 12

Be'ezrat Hashem — with God's help

Bergen Belsen — Nazi concentration camp

Betar — Zionist youth group

Beth Din — Rabbinical law court

Bimah — Raised platform in synagogue

Birchat Hamazon — grace after meals

Brachot — blessings

Bris/Brit Mila — circumcision ceremony

Chagim — festivals

Challah — knotted bread used for Sabbath meal

Channukah — festival of lights, commemorating the victory of the Maccabees

Chassidus — Religious movement emphasising the value of spiritualism, prayer, and faith

Chazzanus/Chazzanut — Liturgical singing

Cheder — religious school

Chuppa — Jewish wedding canopy

Cohanim — priests

Daven — to pray

David Levy — an Israeli politician

Diaspora — Jewish communities outside Israel
ECAJ — Executive Council of Australian Jewry
Frum — religious
Gefilte fish — minced fish balls
Gemara shiur — a lesson in judgements, which forms part of the
     Talmud
Gett — Jewish divorce
Ghetto — areas of townships to which Jews were confined
Giyur — conversion
Habonim (Habo) — Zionist youth movement
Haggada/Hagadot — story of Passover
Hakoah Club — Jewish club in Sydney
Halachah — Jewish law
Hashem — God
JCA — Jewish Communal Appeal
Kashrut — dietary laws (including the separation of meat and milk
     foods, and abstaining from certain kinds of meat, poultry
     and fish
Kehillat Masada — synagogue at Masada College
Kein-ein hara — protection from the evil eye
Kibbutz — cooperative community in Israel
Kiddush — blessing over wine on Shabbat and festivals
Kippah/Kippot — (Yarmulke), scull cap/s
Knesset — Israel's parliament
Kol Nidrei — service on *Yom Kippur* evening
Kolel — Institute for Talmudic study
Kristallnacht — Night of Broken Glass, Germany, 1938
Kurt Waldheim — former UN General Secretary and Austrian
     president (alleged to have been involved in war crimes in the
     Second World War)
Machon — one year educational program in Israel for highschool
     graduates
Magen David — Star of David
Masada College — Jewish school on Sydney's North Shore
Mashiach — Messiah
Matzah — unleavened bread, eaten during *Pesach*

Mezuzot — Torah verses on parchment fixed to the door frames of Jewish house

Mikva — Jewish ritual bath

Mincha — afternoon service

Mitnadev — volunteer

Mitzvah/Mitzvot — good deed/s

Moriah — Jewish school in Sydney

Mosshiach — Messiah

Payes — sidelocks worn by some orthodox Jews

Pesach — (Passover) Festival celebrating the Israelites' exodus from Egypt

Pesach Seder — festive meal on Passover

Pizmonim — poems

Purim — Festival celebrating the failed attempt to destroy the Jews of Persia

Rabbi Brian Fox — Sydney Reform rabbi

Rav — rabbi

Rebbe — spiritual leader of a Chassidic movement

Rosh Hashana — Jewish new year

Seder — festive meal on Passover

Sephardi — Jews of Mediterranean or Asian origin

Shabbat/Shabbos — Sabbath

Shadchan — matchmaker

Shavuot — harvest festival, anniversary of giving of Ten Commandments

Shidduch/Shidduchim — match/es (as in matchmaking)

Shiurim — classes

Shiva — period of mourning

Shmira — security patrolling

Shomrei Shabbat — those who observe to the laws of the Sabbath

Shtetl — small Jewish town in eastern Europe

Shtreimels — round fur hats worn by some ultra-Orthodox Jews

Shul — synagogue

Siddur — prayer book

Smichot — rabbinical ordination

Succa — harvest hut erected for the festival of *Sukkot*.

Sukkot — Festival of Tabernacles

T'fillah — prayer

Talitot/Talitim — prayer shawls

Talmud — Body of oral law, comprising the Mishnah and Gemara

Tefilin — small leather boxes, containing Biblical quotations, placed
on the arm and forehead during morning prayers

Tenach — Hebrew scriptures

Torah — the five books of Moses

Tzitzit — garment worn under the shirts

UIA — United Israel Appeal

Ulpan — Centres in Israel which teach immigrants Hebrew

Wizo — Women's International Zionist Organisation

WUJS — World Union of Jewish Students

Yad Vashem — Holocaust memorial and museum in Jerusalem

Yahrtzeit — anniversary of a person's death

Yehudi — Jew

Yerushalayim — Jerusalem

Yeshiva — Talmudical learning centre

Yiddish — A language similar to Middle German and written in
Hebrew characters, spoken by eastern European Jews

Yiddishkeit — Judaism

Yom Kippur — Day of Atonement

Yom Tov/s — Jewish festival/s